The Book of Fans

by Nancy Armstrong F.R.S.A.

with a Foreword by
Mrs Hélène Alexander
President of the Fan Circle

Designed and Produced by

Ted Smart & David Gibbon

MAYFLOWER BOOKS, INC.,
NEW YORK 10022.

For Sandra, my dearly loved and very talented daughter.

CONTENTS

Foreword

by Mrs Hélène Alexander, President of the Fan Circle

Since the formation of the Fan Circle, Nancy Armstrong and I have been through so many vicissitudes, that I have come to admire this remarkable lady, and am constantly amazed at the scope of her knowledge and her continuing thirst for it.

Her contribution to the World of Fine Arts is undeniable, and her avid research into the sources of her information, has led her to conclusions of value to student and amateur alike.

Her boundless energy in bringing to the layman, as well as to the true connoisseur, visual enjoyment of whichever subject she chooses to speak or write on, makes her one of the most popular lecturers and writers in her field.

Mrs Armstrong is also a practical person, and her advice is always tempered with words of warning.

Perhaps it is because she is such an incurable enthusiast that she so fully understands the problems involved in the preservation and conservation of fine objects. But, it is also because she has actually worked on the repair of fans herself, and because she knows so intimately the contents of the greatest Collections in the World, that she is most qualified to point out to us the many stumbling blocks that occur.

Her personality is such, that most of the World famous Collectors have been delighted with her expertise and unstintingly allowed her to make full use of the unique material in their collections.

It is as a collector, a friend, and a colleague on the Fan Circle, that I am indeed flattered and greatly touched to have been asked to write this Foreword to a book which will bring pleasure and information and food for thought to all its readers.

Hélène Alexander.

Page 1. *Chinese fan, made for the European market, of finely carved, pierced and fretted ivory. c. 1800.*
Page 2. *Chinese fan dated 1873. This was not made for the European market. It is of painted paper with a colophon, bamboo sticks and an inscription on the guards. The reverse has fine calligraphy.*
Pages 4 and 5. *Reverse of German fan dated 1738. Ivory sticks painted with miniatures and guardsticks 'enclouté'.*
Page 7. *Three modern Japanese fans, showing some delicacy of touch in the paintings.*
Pages 8 and 9. *Fan showing a moth painted on silk gauze, with multi-coloured sequins and gold thread. (Possibly painted by George Teiswetter of the Allen Fan Company, Mass., U.S.A.) Sticks of carved and gilded wood. c. 1890.*

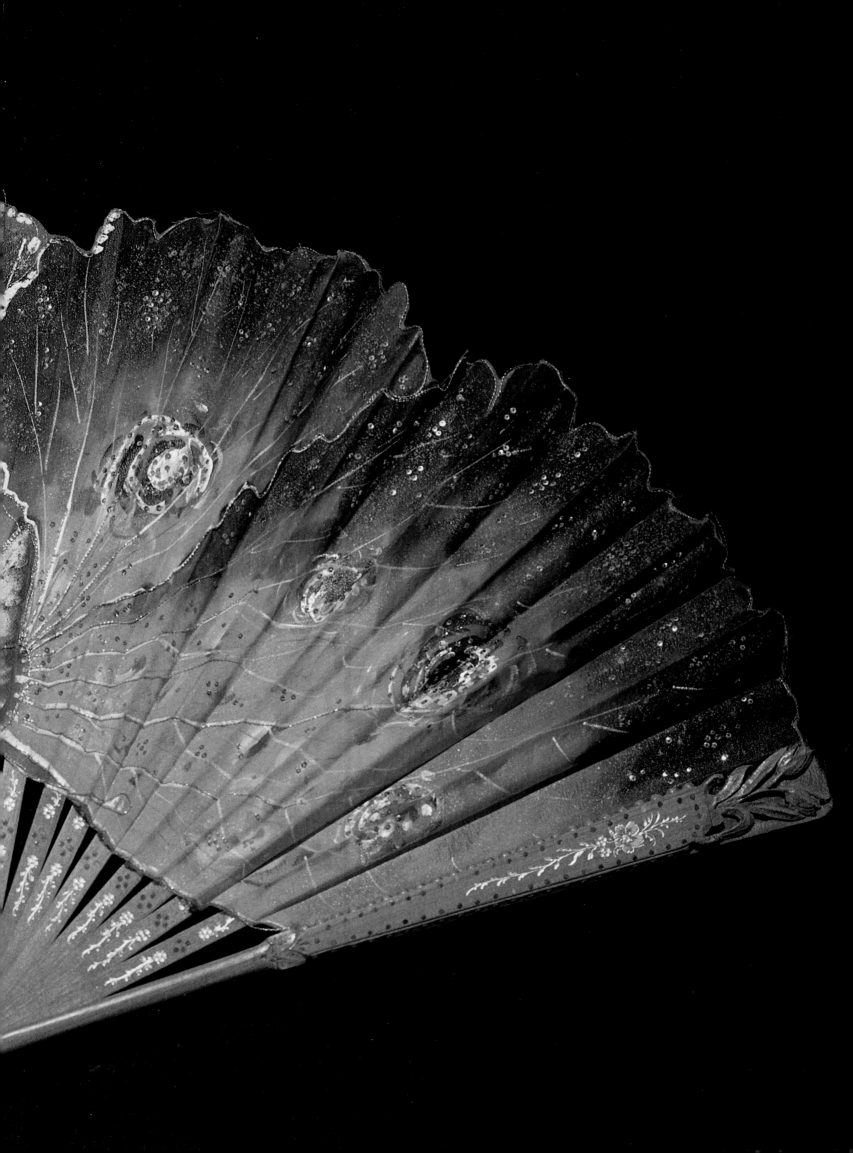

The History of the Fan

How did it all begin, this use of a fan? No-one really knows – except the first person on this earth who felt too hot, picked up a palmleaf to "agitate the air" and cooled him-or herself down.

The word "fan" comes from the latin *vannus,* meaning an instrument for winnowing grain. People all over the world from the dawning of history to the present day have winnowed their grain; there are references to this important task in Greek mythology, the Bible, Shakespeare and dry-as-dust reports from the United Nations.

If grain could be winnowed by a fan then the sweating labourer could cool himself down by using one too. Later this humble instrument had a dozen uses, from hiding the modest blushes of a naked Roman lady in a mixed bath to providing a tiny tray at the Court of Marie Antoinette. To be drawn by a fan one has to have a feeling for work in miniature; to be magnetised by exotic materials from far-away lands which appear blown together by magic rather than worked by mortal fingers; to have an imagination which can clearly visualise the social occasions when the unspoken "language of the fan" was an essential part of passionate feminine nonsense, and a respect for the part a fan has played in various cultures, taking in, for example, the battle fans of Japan, the feather mosaics of Mexico, and the punkahs of India.

Shape, size, treatment, subject-matter and materials all guide the collector today. By studying these features of a fan it is possible to date it and to allocate its country of origin.

China and Japan

All the ancient civilisations of the world have recorded the use of ceremonial fans but the Chinese and Japanese peoples have the longest continuous history of the use of personal fans. Their uses there were carefully proscribed within rigid court etiquette, as well as ordinary social customs and the dance. Perhaps it is as a result of this that fans in the East have always been far more open to variations in technique, material, design and use than, for instance, fashion-conscious France.

Ancient types before the sixth century A.D. were of every variation on the shape of the moon, the pear, the flag and the heart. They used woods, jade, bamboos, basts, turtle-shells, silks, feathers and embroidered textiles; the handles were of iron, gold, silver, ivory, leather or lacquer. The fans were either fixed and rigid or folding – the latter being a technique invented by the Japanese in the seventh century A.D. It is claimed that the Chinese were probably the first to apply a painted design upon a fan.

Early Europe and the Middle East.

In ancient Europe and the Middle East fans started out either as crude instruments, usually intended to whisk away flies, or as large ceremonial standards. The fly-whisk would have been made of grassy reeds turned back on themselves, or bound feathers or animal hairs, of a kind that can still be seen today carried by some rulers and Paramount chiefs in Africa.

The Egyptians sophisticated these crude fans to considerable lengths, and handles became longer as it became traditional to have a slave do the work while his master languished on the couch. Eventually they made huge ceremonial standards to attend their rulers and their consorts, fan and umbrella in one. Two magnificent examples were found in King Tutankhamun's tomb, having gold mounts with embossed and incised decorations fitted up with brown and white ostrich feathers, in one case the handle being of gold and in the other the handle was of ebony overlaid with gold and lapis lazuli. Ritual and religious connotations were not restricted to Egypt; they appeared in most countries in which fans were used, mainly to whisk flies away from the statues of the gods – especially in countries influenced by Indian religions.

At a later date, in the manner the Christian Church often adopted, the pagan tradition of protecting gods from the dirt of flies was sophisticated by the Catholics. They operated a *flabellum* or *ripidia,* a type of fixed fly-whisk, to prevent flies from dropping into the Eucharistic wine and thereby desecrating Christ's blood; this practice continued until the vessels of the service were standardised and the patten acquired a dip in its design which neatly fitted into the top of the chalice, thus shutting out all insects. The flabellum was used roughly from the fifth to the fifteenth centuries and some are extant today and are the property of a church or a museum.

Renaissance Europe.

By the fifth century the liturgical fan was on the wane but the great merchant traders were on the move. The development of the Portugese as a conquering power in the Far East dates from 1497 and the first expedition of Vasco da Gama. He made three other expeditions during the first twenty years of the sixteenth century which firmly established Portugal as a formidable trading power.

Portugese sailors extended their journeys as far as China, and from there to Japan in 1517, returning to Europe with delightfully strange luxuries – these included the folding fan for the use of ladies.

For a century and a half fans were considered as jewelled toys, and both rigid and folding ones were used in the Courts of all Europe. In typical Renaissance splendour they were treated individually, using the rarest available materials and often garnished with precious metals and stones. It is known that feather and tuft fans had occasionally been in use during the four centuries before, made from peacock, ostrich and parakeet feathers arranged in the natural way that they grew, their handles being of carved ivory, gold or jewelled silver, hung from the girdle by a chain.

Now, in the sixteenth century, they were to be taken up and to be used as a fashion accessory by the most sophisticated and advanced women in Europe: the ladies from the great Italian city states.

These cities, lying coincidentally in the paths of returning crusaders, hot, humid and ridden with flies in summer, were ideal for the use of a personal fan. Venice, Milan,

Genoa and Sienna all were known to use slightly differing types; each city was proud of its own individuality, so their dress was identifiably different, so were their accessories, so were their fans.

Some fans made for the queens of the fifteenth and sixteenth centuries cost an immense amount of money, and the traditional makers were the perfumers.

The folding fan travelled up from Italy through France, mainly in the trousseau of Catherine de Medici (1519–89) who made her first public entry into Paris as Queen in 1549; then the fashion for fans exploded into all the other countries in Europe…Elizabeth of England had a great many inventoried in her wardrobe at her death.

By the end of the sixteenth century, as far as we can see from portraits and armorial devices, fans were either made from feathers or from cut-out vellum or thick paper. This cut-out work is called "Decoupé", the design being taken from contemporary Italian lace known as "Reticella", formal and geometrical. One which remains (but has not been seen in public for some years) is the Cluny Museum's fan which traditionally was owned by Henri III of France, Catherine's son; another is a closely similar one from the Oldham Collection, now owned by the Museum of Fine Arts in Boston and exhibited in 1977 – both are illustrated in most fan histories.

From the seventeenth century onwards the fan entered into a completely new role; they were for women; they were for fashion; they were exported from one country to another and from now on they are collectable.

Painted fans.

The quality of European fans produced between the seventeenth century and today depends very much on their painted decorations.

It is generally the case that seventeenth century fans were rather dark in tone, partly because many of them were made from brown leather or thick brownish paper, and over-painted. All the accent was on the leaf and the sticks (of wood, ivory or bone) were left reasonably plain. The leaf took a good three-quarters of the available space, the sticks the remainder, often with round shoulders and overlapping each other.

However there was the tremendous interest on Oriental imports at that time and many Chinese and Japanese lacquered sticks were imported from the East, sometimes made up as fans, sometimes not. Then the Europeans decided to copy the techniques of the East, and the small (because it was expensive) brisé "japanned" fan was made. Therefore there were two types of fans in general use at the turn of the century (into the eighteenth century) the large, spreading painted fan of Europe and the small, original (or copied) brisé japanned fan from the East.

Most of the painted designs were classical or mythological, often showing compositions which were closely copied from the work of a well-known artist in an equally well-known building. This was a rather curious treatment for anything quite as traditionally feminine as a fan – but the *tradition* was born in the mid-eighteenth century, fifty years later; the earlier fans were rather more a question of miniaturising some famous picture of fresco, treating it like an oblong easel painting, then cutting off the corners in a curve (and a convenient space for the sticks) and mounting it onto sticks for use as a fan.

This is also the great period for Biblical scenes and "Triumphs", with the design using up all its "canvas", spreading fully from one side right to the other, generally without a painted border or frame.

Dependent upon the area of its manufacture so the tones of designs ranged darker as you travelled further north, lighter as you travelled to warmer climates, very much following the use of warm tapestries or cooler painted frescoes.

The eighteenth century was the grand age of fans.

Now the painted space was framed by a painted border, broken up into "vignettes" or small individual scenes, treated with every form of inventiveness, and the leaf "married" the sticks in design where possible.

Historical events dominated the designs of many Georgian fans, which had become, by now, a very highly sophisticated business. On the whole they also followed painting styles, styles in dress, and fashions of all the applied arts of the time. This meant, for instance, that when one saw the sticks of fans straightening out, and showing light between them, they were following the furniture designs and leaving behind the heaviness of early eighteenth century baroque.

There was a period from the French Revolution to the first quarter of the nineteenth century when fans stopped being painterly works of art and turned towards the crafts or printed fans. This was to avoid any form of confrontation between the social classes; mistress and maid could afford the same fan at times, and what wealth there was tended to be hidden.

From 1829 there was a revival of painted fans, mostly concentrating on painted textiles and very eclectic in design, copying the glories of the Madame de Pompadour era.

This is where the inexperienced collector can be hoodwinked into buying a Victorian fan, thinking it to be eighteenth century work. But there are clues – painted *white* hair, when Georgian hair powder was grey in tone; sticks which are too thick, gilding which is too brassy, painted scenes which are too crowded…or the inevitable Victorian leaf married to older Georgian sticks which, because of their quality or value, had been kept for a new leaf when the original had worn out or torn. No real attempt at cheating was envisaged most of the time, it was merely a prudent act for the slightly impoverished and no-one ever considered "antiques" (unless they were classical Greek) or the possibility that their intimate possessions would, one day, be sold.

Printed fans.

The fashion for printed fan leaves first arose in England in the 1720's. On examination the earlier printed fans appear both simple and rather crude; the scenes badly drawn and the colours daubed on.

However, matters improved considerably after 1740, and were even better after 1760.

Now the earliest prints are extremely rare for, within a lifespan, printed fans had improved so much that the older ones were destroyed; besides, the subject-matter on each was so ephemeral that the older ones looked old-fashioned – a terrible crime in the Georgian age!

Every type of printed technique was employed, together with colouring. And the subjects were enormously varied. There were maps, amongst many other ideas, almanacks, games, riddles, dances, commemorative and political themes; printed fans provided the most wonderful means to see what people really felt or did or wore at a given moment. They have immense vitality because it is only too obvious that they were entirely "of their time", and they give the viewer the opportunity to look into people's lives and thoughts just as though he was looking through a window.

Almost all printed fan-leaves in Britain have their date of issue on them, together with the name of the publishers, in accordance with the provisions of an Act of 1735. When dates are missing it is not because of an attempt to cheat but because they were cut off to fit the leaf accurately onto the sticks.

Printed fans were made fast and furiously; as each political slogan was altered and a new one came in, so the fan-leaf was torn from its sticks and another slapped on – hence the saying "off with the old, on with the new!"

But after the middle of the 19th century the printed fan, in general, was overtaken by the fans made from textiles, embroideries, laces or feathers.

The lithographed fan (its invention was in 1798) was at its most popular in Europe in the 1840's, especially the highly-coloured and gilded fans from Spain; so care has to be taken to distinguish between printed leaves, lithographed leaves, etched leaves and those which have pen and ink drawings, lightly over-coloured. Their values differ highly.

The death of the fan.

The production of fans began to slow down all over Europe as the rôle of women altered and conventions slackened. After the first world war the fan had fined down to either advertising gimmicks or two slender tinted ostrich feathers on a silver or amber handle.

Young girls would travel, often alone, to the newest event – a "cocktail party". They would wear short skirts, closely fitting hats and drive themselves in a little "runabout". Once they arrived they would transfer their fan and their silver chain-purse to one hand in order to hold a cocktail in the other…and then someone would offer them a cigarette. The most daring would accept, but what would they discard in order to have a free hand?

They discarded the fan.

Nowadays women are listening to health warnings; do not feel they have to make individual "independent" marks and many women can be seen all over the world with fans in their hands again. Some are modern fans, made in Spain or Italy or Oriental countries, some are antique fans bought at auction sales.

A rest of fifty years has done the trick and fans, as throughout time, are again "agitating the air" and cooling people down again. They have also become first-class investments, growing in value faster than almost anything in the antiques world.

Making your collection

I met a traveller from an antique show,
His pockets empty, but his eyes aglow,
Upon his back, and now his very own,
He bore two vast and trunkless legs of stone.
Amid the torrent of collectors' jargon
I gathered he had found himself a bargain,
A permanent conversation piece post-prandial,
Certified genuine Ozymandial
And when I asked him how he could be sure,
He showed me P. B. Shelley's signature.

The atmosphere of the auction rooms is as heady as wine and the avid collector can make the most hideous mistakes unless he is ruthlessly firm with himself.

Who, then, are the collectors? Generally speaking, the Museums of the world, big-time and little-time dealers and private people. It is important, however, to remember that, however much publicity is put out by the major auction houses of the world, whose sales mount up into the hundreds of millions each year, the accepted trade view is that auctions represent only five to ten per cent of total art dealings in the world and the rest are private sales. It is a sobering thought and leaves one to consider the difficulties of authenticity, provenance and conservation.

I recommend *The English as Collectors* by Frank Herrmann (Chatto & Windus 1972) as a brilliant commentary on the general habits and psychology of English collectors. Reading about the extraordinary antics many of our most famous collectors got up to makes one's own idiosyncracies quite tame by comparison.

Read, at the same time, *The Plundered Past* by Karl Meyer (Art Books Society 1973) and then you can comfort yourself that nothing you might ever do would equal some of the shocking actions taken by many of the great world museums.

Frank Herrmann, in his preface, explains that his aim had been to chronicle what was collected, by whom, the source of supply, the transitory nature of private collections, the astonishing survival of family accretions, the growth of expert knowledge, the emergence of permanent public galleries…and, quite incidentally, the gradual transformation of what were once merely articles of domestic decoration into what are now items of considerable financial significance.

Fan collectors have all of this ahead of them. Great paintings, sculpture and architecture have all been well documented, catalogued and attributed to various artists or collections. Most ceramics and furniture of especial note is well-known, and so is the finest gold, silver and jewelry. But what of fans? On this subject we are, quite amazingly, at the threshold of so much discovery. It seems extraordinary that, in the last quarter of the twentieth century we could have such a complete field to chronicle.

Whether one is aware of it or not, Britain is still such a treasure house of art and the decorative arts that all the world envies her. The dealers help to sustain the situation by

buying back into the country objects which might have escaped abroad. But no great fan sales have been permanently shifted to Geneva or Paris from London auction houses as yet, so fine fans are still in our midst and, depending upon certain circumstances (even the deterrent of a heavy shower of rain) alert collectors can pick up a bargain anywhere in the country. Naturally this bargain might have to be put away for some time, but, comparitively speaking, prices are rocketing and it would be rare to make a *bad* purchase today.

"Culture creates collections and collections create culture" – so observed Dillon Ripley, the Secretary of the Smithsonian Institution in Washington. Karl Meyer continues in his book: "The collector, then, is a friend of the past. But he can be a difficult friend. If there is any common trait in all collectors it is the wish to please himself, to create a unique world of objects over which he reigns." He then continues to describe a collection gathered together by a friend of his in Rome which was a mélée of the most beautiful objects ever seen. He goes on to say: "But, for all its enchantment, his collection was of negligible scholarly value because the criterion for his choice was simply what gave him pleasure. This is not said in condemnation, but rather in order to explain why the eclectic style, so prevalent among collectors, limits the value of what is accumulated".

The answer, then, is to specialise. Later, when you make your Will, you should leave the refined collection intact, either for another person with the same interests, or to a museum.

Museum staff are nearly always helpful as they have an obvious commitment to the public. Very often the Curator of a museum is a frustrated collector, yet every Curator is more than aware that every collector is a potential donor to his museum – which occasionally makes the Curator more ruthless than the collector. However, museum staff generally hear through the grapevine of the availability of a treasured fan long before the public, and can advise on its purchase if the museum does not need it, thus cutting out the middleman or the auction house. A fine collection, too, might be just what a museum is seeking and would

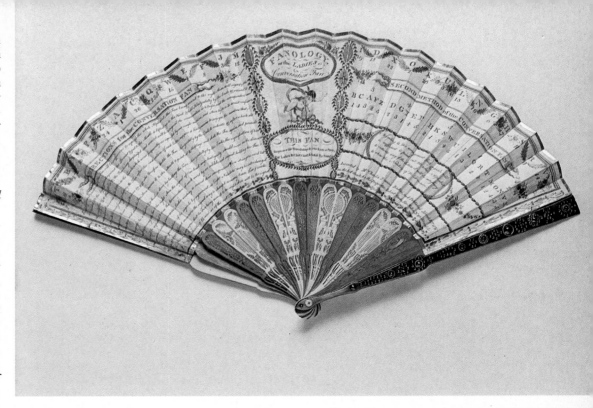

Left. *A very fine Oriental ivory cockade fan reminiscent of frozen lace.*
Top right. *"Fanology" published by Robert Clarke in 1797 and designed by Charles Francis Badini. The sticks are of ivory and sandalwood. The central cartouche says: "The Fan improves the Friendship, and sets forth a Plan; For Ladies to Chit-Chat and hold the tongue." Originally owned by Lady Charlotte Schreiber, her handwriting on the box was recognised, quite by chance, by her great-grandson, Lord Oranmore and Browne, at a sale. Photo: Michael Stannard.*
Centre right. *"A Grape Harvest". c. 1750. A fine Viennese fan of vellum, with ivory sticks, carved and painted. Photo: Michael Stannard.*
Bottom right. *An advertising fan of high quality. Silk gauze is embroidered with gold sequins and spangles, with a gilded coat of arms in the centre and the words "Metropole Hotel". Gilded bone sticks and guards. c. 1890.*

buy from the effects of a well-known collector, as long as it is a specialised collection.

It is wise to remember that there are rules for the collector and different rules for the Museums of this world. Hanging over our heads are various laws and taxes and it is the duty of the collector to have available all information about their purchases in case the law needs to know more of your affairs, depending upon the country in which you live. These rules of disclosure do not apply to all Museums in the same way and it is difficult to crack the nut, officially, of the provenance of a new acquisition, the dealer through whom it was bought and the price paid for it – especially in America. So, for your own protection, keep the most meticulous details about all purchases and any other fan you may have seen, either in a Museum or another collection, which seems similar to your own or appears to come from the same category e.g. Jewish painted fans from Amsterdam, all possibly from the same workshop.

In 1970 there was a meeting in Paris of Museum authorities to discuss the question of the ethics of museum acquisition, sponsored by the International Council of Museums. The collector, too, is faced with one or two questions on ethics when making a collection. Firstly, whether or not to buy a fan without a pedigree? The saleable fan might come through private hands – but where is your proof that the fan is not stolen? Ethically-minded collectors must preserve their sense of responsibility on this subject, especially if the International Foundation for Art Research (founded New York 1968) really gets into its stride. The concern of this body of people is to gather information and, eventually, to evolve into a multinational clearing-house for computer data; and for descriptions of lost, stolen and plundered arts of all kinds. I feel that this should also, one day, be the responsibility of the Fan Circle – to feed their information into the I.F.A.R. computer bank and so help to preserve fine fans in the world.

Secondly there are the ethics of conservation. As Karen Finch said (lecture to the Royal Society of Arts on 10th November 1976 on "Textile Conservation"): "An object should leave the hands of the conservator with all clues to its past history intact or fully recorded, or the work – and the word – will have no meaning." She then went on to discuss the various stages of the techniques used at the Textile Conservation Centre in London and added: "One aspect (of our work) is the documentation and recording of the information that may be contained in every piece of work and which sometimes is revealed only by the work we do in conservation…in all fields of conservation *irreversible* work would close the door to the past and further research into our artistic, social and technological history."

It is more than evident that conservation is the co-operative product of the scientist working with the historian – and that there are simply not enough ethical conservationists in the world. Their trouble is lack of money to pay their dedicated workers, with the inevitable result that one finds a few overworked amateur or semi-professional repairers at large. They do not, in the main, aim to deceive or even to fleece their clients, but then they never even pretend to be conservationists either. I have written on repairing fans in this book, using all the conservationists' materials, but at no time have I suggested that the advice is for anything other than *repairs*. Yet, without this advice – the first ever given to fan collectors, and the work of the fan repairers – how else could we prevent even more fans falling into rot and decay?

No country gives sufficient money towards conserving their own treasures – some give nothing at all – and, when looking towards the example set by the authorities in Mexico or Italy or Asia, we are daily faced with the chilling phrase: "the past has no future unless we are willing to pay for it." As fan collectors let us always couple the word conservation with collecting, and, if we cannot afford conservation treatment on our fans, let us – at the very least – keep them in good repair.

Frauds are universal in all the arts and many a great Museum has mistakenly bought, for huge sums of money, some colossal mistake. They make these dreadful mistakes because there are such able forgers and fakers about and yet, as far as we all know, there has never been a deliberate fraud over a fan. That is not to say that, during the nineteenth century various copies (rather than fakes) of eighteenth century fans were not made – we know they were and we also know how to tell the difference (e.g. painted *white* hair, rather than grey, in a Georgian scene etc.,) but, during the last ten years no-one has come across deliberate faking of valuable fans.

It is quite possible that there will be frauds in the future: inevitably there must be, as the prices of fans rise. Mr Hoving, formerly of the Metropolitan Museum of New York once said that "the tension of apprehension over the authenticity of anything for sale was a normal part of Museum work. It takes study

Left. *Cockade fan of painted silk with a lace border, made up on ivory sticks which fasten together. c. 1750. Possibly Dutch.*
Right. *A selection of English Regency horn fans, three with barrel rivets. The sticks were placed in moulds, plunged into boiling water (which softened them and made them translucent – known as 'greenhorn') and, when cool, the designs were painted on. The fan at the top was for a doll.*

and expertise to prove that something is good, but at the same time you have to watch very carefully that you don't commit the sin of branding something a falsehood when it is, in fact, a genuine piece." Museums have their problems, with all their great experts to hand, so the average collector is even further out on a limb. It is this very isolation which must make the collector especially careful not to buy a good fan without a pedigree from a stranger or through an untested source. It is often difficult to prove one's good intentions, and buying and selling fakes, forgeries or stolen goods, even unwittingly, carries a jail sentence.

The most important single attribute of a great collector, as always in the past, is an eye for quality. The second most important attribute is an impeccable attitude towards provenance. The thought that an enlightened enthusiast can pick up a great work for a few shillings is what spurs on many people. It does happen, and, unlike the major arts, it can happen rather more often than one would imagine…yet this is going to become increasingly rare. With all the work that is now going into fan history, the wider diffusion of knowledge is making it less possible to discover significant fans that are either underrated or overlooked.

It may be more important to pay the right price at the right time. In a market where the demand is steadily increasing and the supply must of its very nature dwindle, prices are always on the increase, particularly for the pieces which are genuinely what they claim to be. A fully documented sales or collecting history, a pedigree or provenance, is probably as reliable a guide to authenticity as any other. If fan collectors will always concentrate on this aspect of provenance the final amalgam of flair, taste, fashion, patronage and financial acumen will make fans an even more fascinating subject, and which will gradually establish itself as an important aspect of our social history.

Who, then, are the fan collectors? With the threat of the Wealth Tax hovering overhead it would be mad disloyalty to mention any living collector's name, although they are obvious enough at the auction sales. These people today, bidding in their own names and not through agents, have collections which are, in the main, in embryo.

But what of the past? Only one name stands out from the nineteenth century in Europe as being so important that her collection is used as a yardstick of identification today by the auction houses – Lady Charlotte Schrieber.

Fortunately a good deal of initial work has been done on various other collections and catalogues are beginning to appear. The Victoria and Albert Museum has been working hard on their collection, so has the Costume Museum in Bath. The York Castle Museum's collection has recently been catalogued by Mrs Pat Clegg and Mrs Alexander, President of the Fan Circle; the Rothschilds' collection at Waddesden is now recorded; Mrs Emily Joy has written up the Bristols' collection at Ickworth; Mr Felix Tal's collection is well-recorded; Miss Esther Oldham's collection has now gone to the Boston Museum of Fine Arts and let us hope

there will, in time, be a catalogue of the famous Messel collection owned by the Countess of Rosse. So it goes on, with articles written in various journals by authors such as Therle Hughes, Mary Gostelow, Hélène Alexander, Everna Zabell and others, giving the auction houses plenty of further material from which to work and use as yardsticks.

Lady Charlotte Schrieber was legendary for her remarkable intellectual capacity, her scholarship and her fantastic energy. She collected a huge variety of objects, specialising on ceramics, lace, playing cards and fans. Her knowledge of fakes and forgeries was encyclopaedic and she had an iron will, buying only if she thought the price was right. Fortunately Lady Charlotte kept copious notes and eventually her son, Montague Guest, published a selection from her journals of the years 1869–1885. He also, (in c.1909) wrote an extremely interesting introduction to her works, pointing out the almost total lack of knowledge and interest in "antiques" in Lady Charlotte's days. In the 1860's onwards (antique-collecting became an Edwardian phenomenon) everyone was wanting things which were either "new" or "machine-made", and they threw out, or sold for a song, items of the past. No-one knew, or cared, about Chelsea or Bow, Sheraton or Hepplewhite, and so Lady Charlotte had a clear field and gleefully scooped the pool.

She learned by trial and error: she had to…with no written help. She was an avid reader and studied French, German, Italian, Greek, Latin, Hebrew, Persian and ancient Welsh and she also travelled extensively. She was born in 1812, the only daughter of the 9th Earl of Lindsey (there were two sons) and, when she was twentyone she married Sir John Guest, who was twice her age. Twenty years later she was widowed and, three years later, she created an uproar by marrying the tutor to her children, Charles Schrieber. From then on she travelled Europe with her husband, searching for china, not really having become interested in the subject until she was over fifty years old.

Very soon Lady Charlotte realised that buyers of old china were at the mercy of the seller's jargon and tales, rather than real facts. So she decided to go to the sources and went through the catalogues and account books of various manufactures and began a serious and scholarly collection. The Victoria and Albert Museum were the beneficiaries of a good deal of her collection after the death of her husband in 1884; there were just over 1800 items of porcelain, earthenware, glass and enamels.

As remarked earlier, Lady Charlotte was also an avid collector of lace, playing cards and fans, and during the last four years of her life she supervised the production of two immense series of catalogues of her extensive collections: the first of fans and fan-leaves and the second of playing cards. She also bequeathed both of these collections to the British Museum after her death in 1895. Fortunately Lady Charlotte had over forty grandchildren at her death, for she left a quite incredible amount of objects to them (Lord Oranmore and Browne is a great grandson). She seemed to travel through Europe as an erudite vacuum-cleaner,

enjoying herself hugely all the while. For example, in 1869 she was in Italy touring, until she had exhausted the local shops and private collections, dashing into churches and factories, mixing art, erudition and straight, hard bargaining with ruthless efficiency. Sometimes she searched for an object, sometimes she spotted a bargain and on many other occasions she fumed with rage that various dealers could take her for an idiot, which, clearly, she was not. Luckily for her she was sufficiently rich to be able to say "no" when it suited her, perhaps picking up some purchase on "the second time round" in some sales room, and she seemed to have both an unerring eye and a limpit-like tenacity travelling side by side together with a quite amazing stamina.

"Venice. June 1869. On Friday 25th, we went over to Torcello, taking Murano on our way and again visiting Zanetti and the Museum, a delightful excursion. On our return went through Burano. Enquired there about lace, and found one old woman making a little, but it was very coarse, bad stuff. Our enquiries were first made in a respectable, but humble dwelling (glittering, however, with brazen utensils) which we found to belong to the village tailor. His wife, a pretty young woman, who was tending twins in two cradles, not only received and directed us courteously, but insisted on our returning (after seeing the Church) to partake of coffee. The Burano people exhibit a taste I have not seen elsewhere, arranging their gaily coloured earthenware plates and dishes against the walls of their houses on racks which are constructed in pyramidical form. All the Islands seem very poor, but this is the best of them.

Amongst the interesting sights of Venice I must not forget the Scoule of San Rocco, San Giovanni, and San Marco, the public Gardens (where the lime flowers were just going out of bloom) and the Lido. Also numberless excursions around the City, the Giudecca, etc. The name of our gondolier, Luigi Moloso, No. 129. Hotel, Pension Suisse.

On the morning of Saturday 26th, we got up early and went for the day to Padua, remaining there till evening, a most charming expedition. We spent a very long time in the Giotto Chapel, and visited the Churches of S. Antonio (well-remembered for the Marble Boys supporting the candelabra, in 1838) and of Sta. Giustina. We fell in with a little antiquaire, Celin. He had nothing himself, but he took us to others. At another little shop we bought a pair of striped cups and saucers, Venetian, 50c, and a Persian pot and cover, $1.20.

I had been enquiring for lace at Venice and found it awfully dear. La Pompeia has the best selection. Some of it very fine, but extravagant. For a flounce like one bought last year by Ivor she wanted $400. Of course this was out of the question. Happening to mention lace to Celin, he took us to a draper's shop, the master of which Barzilla brought out a series of bundles to show us. Among them was a flounce of near 20 yards, 14 inches deep (very nearly resembling Ivor's, for which he had given $250). To our astonishment we were only asked $64 for it. The flounce was not to be resisted, even in the light of an investment, at that price, so we bought it.

After this we went to the house of 'Giuseppe Bassani, San Cassiano'. He had some very fine things which we promised to visit again; from him we got a Venetian fruit basket and stand, $1.75. From Barzillai 4 Venetian cups and saucers, Japanese pattern, 40c. A moulded cream ware tray (qy. Treviso), $2. When we had completed our purchases, the jovial Barzillai asked us to stay and dine with him, which diverted us vastly. The following Monday, Lady Arbuthnot came to see our lace with Mme Usedom and Mr Trevelyan (the latter a great judge) and they pronounced it wonderful, both as to quality and to price. This (Monday 28th) was our last day at Venice. We took a sorrowful farewell, devoutly hoping ere long to return to it.

29th June. Up at 3. Left Venice at 6…."

Lady Charlotte's eye for detail makes Venice come to life in a wonderfully clear way; late June must have been so hot in Victorian dresses, but there is never a murmur about discomfort during her stay there. Day after day she bought small objects for reasonable sums of money. On 2nd June she bought a Rubens portrait of a man for $54. For other items she only paid cents. But she went everywhere, she saw everything, she explored all the shops and consulted all the dealers and she bought about half a dozen items a day. Yet the main thing which shines out as clearly as the eye of envy was that she enjoyed it all so much and that is the mark of a true collector.

It is interesting that she rarely paid more than $10 for a fan, and was never above having a fan delivered to her, for sale at five shillings, and returning it to the dealer as being unsuitable. It is also interesting to see how high she would go for lace – about which more in another section.

To give a perfect example of thorough research there is a very interesting historical fan, known as the "Dr Sacheverell Fan" which has many sides which would fascinate collectors.

Firstly it is owned by the Right Honourable Lord Oranmore and Browne, great-grandson of Lady Charlotte Schrieber, the most famous collector of the Victorian age; secondly it was made during the first few years of the formation of the Guild of the Worshipful Company of Fan Makers, who received their Charter in 1708, and thirdly it is voluminously documented.

Lord Oranmore and Browne has taken these extracts himself from the catalogue of Prints and Drawings in the British Museum, Division 1, Political and Personal Satires, Vol.11. June 1869 to 1733. Under "Anne", page 307:

An Historical Emblematical Fan in HONOUR OF THE CHURCH OF ENGLAND, and of Such Her Pious and GENUINE SONS, that with Primitive Bravery have suffer'd for and DEFENDED her Holy DOCTRINE in the most perilous Times. As also ENBLEMATICALLY setting-forth the Base Attempts Practised and ABORTIVE Hopes of the Church's Secret and Declar'd ENEMIES. ALL here is adapted to the present happy turn of things. 1711.

(March 20th, 1710)

An engraving of a crescent form as if made for use on a lady's fan. Below is the following MS:-

"EXPLANATION."

"On the Right side of this Fan is St. Pauls Church standing upon a Rock, an EMBLEM of the Church of England, in Allusion to those words of Our Saviour, Upon this Rock will I build my Church. The Queen as head is represented in a circle of laurels, supported by two Angels. The Eye of Providence watching over the Church and Queen. A Dove with an Olive branch flying towards the Church. The Six Bishops (1) and Dr. (2) represents the Bishops and Subordinate Clergy of the Church of England, standing in a discoursing posture. Just by these are the Seven Glorious Martyrs (viz) The Royal Martyr (3), Archbishop Laud and the five Bishops Martyrs (4) in the Marian Reign, as rising out of their Tombs who tho' dead yet speak. On the top of the Rock the standard of Great Britain display'd. On one side is his Grace the Duke of Ormond and the Right Honble. Wm. Bromley Speaker of the present House of Commons on horseback representing the Nobility and Gentry of the Church of England subduing an Hydra lurking at the foot of the Sacred Rock. Opposite to this is a figure representing the Mouth of Hell casting fire and darts against the Church. Upon the sea is a boat fitted out with the French Arms and an Owl with a double face in an Oliverian Escutcheon for the colour (5). The Pope is steersman and one of the Boats Crew (6), distinguished by a sprig of Nightshade in his cup, dischargeth a Mortar Piece at the Rock, but one of the Guardian Angels with a flaming sword reverberates the Bomb upon themselves, which at breaking oversets the Boat. In the water is a Crocodile swimming away with a bone in his throat (7). On the sands is a house built, which on the Rains descending and Winds blowing falls; the Jesuit creeping out of a hole sticks fast, the others escape the best they can. In the Forest is a Lyon surpris'd a Wolf in Sheeps cloathing and he disrobeth the Imposture and the Sheep escape, – On the wither'd Stalk of a Tree is a Camelion famous for its changeing colours. The last figure is King David playing upon his Harp to the deaf Adder, which represents the happyness of Retirement." 19 x 6½ in.

1. See Portraits of Six Bishops and Dr. Sacheverell (No 3) March 20, 1710 No 1524.

2. Dr. Sacheverell who is in the middle of the group and evidently the object of episcopal admiration. An angel is about to place a mitre on his head.

3. Charles 1.

4. Cranmer, Latimer, Ridley and Farrar; see "Martyrdom of Reformers" No 10 and "Faiths Victorie in Romes Creveltie" No 10.

5. i.e. the standard or flag which is displayed at the stern of the boat in which three personages are represented.

6. This person is dressed half as a Bishop, with bands and lawn sleeves, half as a Puritan, with a short coat; it was probably intended for Burnet, Bishop of Salisbury or Hoadley, although the latter was not then a bishop; see "a British Janus" 1709 No 1505.

7. It may be but only the tail of the animal is visible.

Back of the Fan.

Extract from catalogue in British Museum:

No 1526.

The LILLIES AMONG THORNS; An Emblem of the Church Militant. A design made for the back of a fan.

(March 20, 1710)

This engraving is executed on the back of the design which is described in this catalogue as "An Historical Emblematical Fan" etc. March 20th 1710 No 1525. It is accompanied by the following in MS.

"The Explanation"

"The Lillies among thorns; an Emblem of the Church Militant. The Grove of Palms with Crowns of Glory, streaming upon them, and over them is a figure of the New Jerusalem; are to signify the rewards reserved in Heaven for the Persevering Rightuous." The fan is reproduced in Gila Curtis' *The Life and Times of Queen Anne* (Weidenfield and Nicholson) 1972 at pp.172,173.

The six divines surrounding Dr. Sacheverell are those who voted for his acquittal at his trial for impeachment in the House of Lords in March 1710. They are the Archbishop of York; the Bishops of London, Durham, Rochester, Bath and Wells, and Chester: see Geoffrey Holmes *The Trial of Dr. Sacheverell* (Eyre Methuen, 1973 Appr B). The house in the background *may* be Dr. Burgess' in Carey Street and the figure round the back of the house Burgess himself.

No one should ever fear putting a fan into a sale at one of the famous auction houses in London; you can expect courtesy, expertise, advice and an all-round professional approach, however modest your fan. It would, however, be wise to attend one or two sales in advance, just to get a feel over the pre-view, the catalogue descriptions and the rapidity of the sale itself. You may, quite easily, decide not to sell but to buy instead!

How *can* one judge what price a fan will bring? It is extremely difficult to say. Quality, rarity, the state of repair and the accuracy of its provenance seem to head the list of qualifications; secondly comes the value of the materials and finally, its age.

Western European fans are most favoured especially where there is mica-work or when there is fine painting on vellum or chicken-skin, and where there is intricate working on sticks and guards, which carry out a similar theme to the design on the leaf. Curiosities come second, such as German articulated fans of the eighteenth century or cyphers of Royal owners on the guards mounted in rose-diamonds etc. Mounted Oriental fans come next in appeal and price, with Chinoiserie running them close. Spanish fans, mainly because of their rather coarse materials (often bone instead of ivory, many sticks being carved in the Philippines for the Spanish leaves) come next in popularity, followed by nineteenth century lace fans, late Victorian and Edwardian ostrich feather fans and finally printed and advertising fans. The list is over-simplified, but it gives a rough guide.

But when you go to buy, beware of cased fans! The case might be more valuable than the fan! Most fans are sold singly, which means one can see both sides and often can handle the fan as well. On the other hand

some fans are locked away in glazed cases. Does that automatically mean the fan is superior? It could do so, especially if there is only a leaf and no sticks, for then the buyer can judge the quality of the painting alone. On the other hand many a bad fan has been bought in the past purely for its case rather than the contents.

Cases come in many shapes and sizes: glazed, lacquered, gesso and gilt, mahogany, glazed on both sides and so on. It would be of interest to know exactly how often an owner turns a fan around when it is framed in a double glazed case. Most fans have an important obverse side and a simple reverse, so it would be almost pointless to change over unless the owner was worried about the effect of light on the fan and wanted to even up the amount of exposure on textiles, vellum or ivory. But, in the main, a fan is seen from one favourite side, so a case which has only one glazed side is sufficient.

The snag at sales is that it is impossible to

Above. *"A Louis XV mother-of-pearl fan, overlaid with cupids and scrollwork in gold, the mount painted with Hercules, Omphale and Cupids."* This description was printed at the time of the Great Red Cross Sale of April 1916, when the fan was sold as part of the collection of the Viscountess Hambleden, formerly in the collection of Lady Holland.

Centre left and bottom left. *"The Mail Arriving at Temple Bar".* Painted by C.B. Newhouse and engraved by J. Bailey. The fan-leaf is a very early state of the plate, the print itself is a very late state. The fan-leaf has obviously been extended at the sides and it is possible that it was rejected as unsaleable. English – 1834. This is a tantalising method of buying prints and fan-leaves.

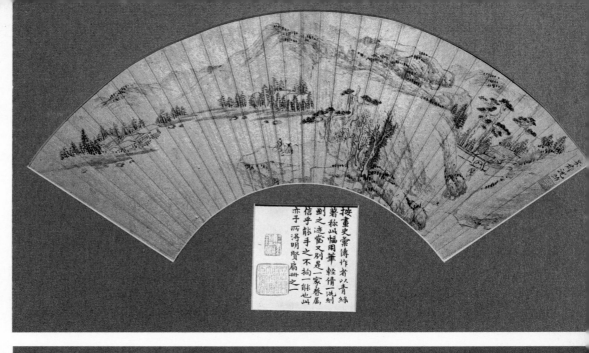

take the fan out, hold it, look at the reverse and find out, for sure, whether there is anything wrong with the fan. A judicious stitch here, an invisible thread there, a carefully backed broken mother-of-pearl guard or a neat layer of new paint might be disguising some real – even disastrous – fault within a fan that otherwise one would have seen outside a case.

But, should you buy a cased fan for the case alone you must be equally careful about shapes and measurements; your own fan, waiting to be put in, might be the right measurement but completely the wrong shape. On the other hand, fans in their original shaped boxes are much sought after. What then, has been the development of fan sales during the last seven years? There have been radical alterations during these years and, it cannot be denied, the advent of three books in English in three years has completely altered the scene for fan buyers and collectors. Amongst other advantages is the increase of either one or two sales of fans for each auction houses a year in 1970 to about twenty in each in 1978. Catalogues are immeasurably better and fans are almost always sold singly nowadays, rather than in lots of up to ten fans at a time, and many are photographed.

In London, in October 1970, there were 228 fans sold in a total of only eighty two separate Lots. They sold for a total of $4,436, which makes an average of just over $18 a fan. The cheapest was a Lot of five fans, one being a lithographed Spanish fan of the late nineteenth century, and *four others*, selling for a grand total of $2. The most expensive was "A magnificent Neo-classical fan, the chicken-skin leaf painted in the style of Zucci with a fine vignette of Thetis arming Achilles, a frieze of ships, with blue and white grisaille panels of classical figures, supported by putti and pillars with draped urns between them, and decorated with sequins, the reverse painted with a woman on a terrace, landscape vignettes and allegories of music, the ivory sticks carved, pierced and backed to simulate jasper medallions of ships – *probably Italian, late 18th century – 9½ in.*" This was bought by a very well-known collector (and member of the Fan Circle) for $640 and is illustrated (No. 7) in Nancy Armstrong's *"A Collectors History of Fans".*

In Geneva (April 30th 1974) there was a sale of "Fans, objects of vertu and decorative and Indian jewellery". Understandably, to raise the prices, one especial section was kept separate, as the objects in it had been the property of the late Queen Victoria Eugenia of Spain, and was being sold by an heir.

Above. *The "Dr Sacheverell Fan". c. 1710. English. Photo: Michael Stannard.*
Overleaf. *Chinoiserie Fan, French, 18th century. Known as "Eventail de grand envol". The leaf of silk embroidered in gold thread in tambour stitch, with spangles, outlining a Chinoiserie design in the manner of Boucher. The baroque ivory sticks are carved, pierced, silvered and gilded.*

There were twenty seven fans which fetched altogether 27,370 Swiss francs (about $12,800). To interest the collector there were seven special photographs, presumably the seven which were estimated to fetch the highest prices and yet – such is the bagatelle of sales – four other fans sold for as much, or more, than the illustrated fans.

Another group of eighteen fans in the same sale fetched 29,150 Swiss fancs (about $14,000). In this case the illustrations showed eight fans which, quite accurately, fetched the highest prices – one fan fetched 7,000 Swiss francs (about $3,200). It is interesting to discover why it fetched so high a price. After all, the leaf was of paper, the sticks of mother-of-pearl and the date c.1860. Was it for the diamonds on the guard? Or because it was owned by the stylish Empress Eugenie?

A full description in the catalogue was:-
"A fine fan, the paper leaf with a central reserve painted with a lady holding a parrot with four other ladies in a landscape within a scrolling gilt frame, accompanied on either side by a cartouche containing a flying putto, the space in between filled with gilt foliage and coloured flowers, *signed C. Roqueplon*, the reverse painted with a flying Cupid in a surround of gilt scrolls and foliage, the sticks pierced and carved with a scene representing the Imperial couple and their court *signed A. Touise* (?), backed with transparent tinted mother-of-pearl, both guard sticks carved with a muse in a niche, a putto holding a medallion and two putti holding a crown. The medallion on the front guard contains the gold initials of the Emperor and the Empress set with rose with rose-diamonds – *29cm, French, circa 1860.* Provenance: Empress Eugenie."

A third group, in the same sale, showed 19 fans, and fetched 11,450 Swiss francs (about $5,400), of which the highest price was 1600 Swiss francs for a German nineteenth century fan and the lowest was 250 Swiss francs for an early nineteenth century French vellum fan.

In August 1975, in London, there was a sale at Christies with twenty-five Lots, of which eight were composite. The total sum for the sale was $1,884, an average of $74 for each Lot; there were, in total, fifty fans altogether, making the average, per fan, of about $37.

In August 1976, in a similar sale, there were fifty-six Lots sold, totalling $4,314, which makes an average of just over $76 per Lot. The lowest price was $20, the highest $420 and four fans sold for $200 or more. It was an average August sale where most great collectors were out of London.

Now Christies were prepared to give a list of estimated prices in advance, to help the buyer, such as $80–$100 for "A fan, the leaf painted with four vignettes, the reserves with vines and shells, the ivory sticks pressed, pierced, painted and backed with tinsel – *10½ in circa 1760*" where, in fact, the fan sold for $16.

On the other hand "A fan, the black kid leaf painted with Gods and Godesses, the reserves and reverse with flowers, the ivory sticks carved and pierced – *12½ in. circa 1695*" was estimated to sell for $160–$200 and actually sold for $420.

There were twenty-five occasions in this sale, out of fifty-nine Lots, where the estimated price was achieved, sometimes at the lowest and sometimes at the highest price. In the other cases some fans went well above the estimated price ($420 rather than $160–$200) and in others well below the estimated price ($40 rather than $70–$90).

The authorities arranging the sale knew exactly what they were doing, had managed dozens of sales before and personally gone through hundreds of Lots – so why was the proportion of estimated prices so wrong? Because of the people who were present, because of what they wanted, that day, to fill

a gap in their collection and because the permutation and combination of buyers, needs, competitors and foibles can never be constant. The fun of an auction sale is just this – the luck of the draw, on that day, during that moment in time.

In seven years, therefore, we can see that the average price of a fan has risen from $18 to $76, with top prices rising from about $640 to $1,900. The latter was "A fan, the leaf set with mother-of-pearl panels painted with Gods, mortals and putti, the reverse painted with a figure in a landscape, the ivory sticks carved and pierced – *10 in. French circa 1760*, in 19th century fitted case."

Fans are now more often sold singly, rather than in Lots, and the catalogue details have improved enormously. All the names of the buyers were included in the price-lists after the sales until 1975, when sales houses only printed the prices and not the buyers' names. So now, unless you attend the sale personally and know the bidders (or for whom they are bidding) one does not know the present-day collectors.

Suddenly the sale of fans has entered the big league and, for fan historians and avid collectors alike, the need will be to attend all the previews and the sales, to mark in one's own catalogue the buyers' names and to record when known fans change hands. The easiest way to get additional information is to attend any of the Fan Circle gatherings and chat, informally, with other collectors; this way one hears about the fans various collectors are looking for, and also when a collector has decided to specialise in one field and is liable to sell the remainder of his collection. Many a fan has quietly changed hands without going through an intermediary.

In order to bring this section up to date it is worth recording a significant sale on the 4th of May 1978. Christies, South Kensington, had a "Sale of an Important Collection of Fans", the property of Mrs August Uihlein Pabst formed by her mother Mrs George B. Baldwin. Christies invited members of the Fan Circle to a Soiree the evening before, where drinks and food were served and all allowed to examine the exhibits of the next day.

On the day of the sale most people came early and quite a few had to stand; there were buyers from the Fan Circle, various Museums and private individuals from France, Germany and Japan amongst others.

There were merely 126 single Lots of fans, plus a book or two and a selection of magazine cuttings etc to make up the last four Lots. There was also an extremely interesting set of estimated prices.

The lowest total for the entire sale was estimated at $31,730; the highest expected was $47,400. In the end of a most exciting sale the total fetched $66,236 (over double the lowest estimate) with an average price of about $540 for each fan.

In this sale two most especial fans stood out. One was a "Mask Fan" or "Beggar's Opera Fan", selling at $4,200 almost the same as Miss Esther Oldham's bequest to the Museum of Fine Arts in Boston. The other was "A fan, the gauze leaf decorated overall with mica painted with vignettes of La Vie Rustique, the ivory sticks gilt and the guardsticks of tortoiseshell clouté with mother-of-pearl and coloured marbles 11½ in. French, circa 1680", which reached an all-time high in Britain for an European fan of $5,200.

It was a fascinating sale, showing the tremendous growing interest in fans since 1970 where, as has been stated, the average price for a fan was $18 and by 1978 the average price had leapt to $540.

The owners of existing collections must be congratulating themselves on their taste and perspicacity over anticipating future trends; their own collections are now worth so very much more in so short a period. But there is still plenty of room for the beginner.

European Fans

The collector today is faced with a reserved selection of types which he or she can find in sales houses; rarely do exciting fans from Burma or American Indians become catalogued in London, nor do very many early seventeenth century ones. As for the sixteenth century, they are never discovered at all. So one can specialise in late seventeenth century fans or fan-leaves and then through to the present day. In view of this it is pointless to detail what might have been but to give as much information as possible on the fans available.

Prices vary wildly; I have made a thorough list of estimated prices, actual prices and prices which appear to have been for twin fan types which have varied as much as from $6 up to $160 for a sandalwood fan with painted decorations. Quality cannot be properly described in a sale catalogue, a "fine fan", an "interesting fan", an "usual fan" will all do justice to the object but, as seen in two catalogues, "an unusual painted sandalwood fan" fetched $6 and "a fine painted sandalwood fan" fetched $160. The answer is that one always has to see for oneself and hope that the weather or Wimbledon tennis fortnight has kept away some of the other collectors that day.

Many people wish to begin their collection with as wide an assortment as possible, behaving like magpies with every type. It happens to be a very sound way to approach fan-collecting because, after some years, you suddenly realise that you have favourites. On looking at them with care it is obvious that, for entirely personal reasons, a certain type of fan attracts you more than the others. There is a well-known collector who specialises in Victorian fans, another collects advertising fans, yet another prefers French eighteenth century painted fans; partly because of personal taste and partly because of prices. Museums attempt to get a representative collection of all known types and materials but the beginner can start off and buy a cheaply priced lot at a sale and go on from there without breaking the bank. There are absolutely no rules.

An alphabetic list of collectable fans from Europe is as follows:-

Advertising

It is quite extraordinary how many types of advertising fans there are for sale – Mr Martin Willcocks and Mrs Everna Zabell are, at present, collating a list of differing types. Most of these fans were made as give-away gifts by inns, stores, hotels, airlines, drinks manufacturers and firms making luxury goods. As they are given away they have to be cheap (one or two are surprisingly expensive) with wooden sticks and paper leaves or mounts.

They are very visual and have P.R. impact well in advance of contemporary advertising in newspapers and journals. Some even have scent-impregnated mounts or, like Rimmel, they even give away a small bottle of their scent in a white cardboard box together with the lacy fan.

They come in every size and shape (one fascinating type is for cocktail olives with a long handle of bamboo and with a tiny folding fan at the top, about an inch wide and brilliantly coloured) and the praiseworthy Willcocks-Zabell collaboration has unearthed about one hundred and fifty types.

Luckily they are still reasonably priced; dealers feel that anything made from paper, with wooden sticks, are too cheap to fetch a sale. Christies have been known to sell ten advertising fans for a total of $12. So there are opportunities here for a good start with a kind of fan which will rapidly increase in value as soon as people realise how interesting they are.

Besides, they show contemporary history in a way which is surprising – one fan shows Piccadilly Circus (at present apparently being demolished) with the Piccadilly Hotel occupying the entire site of Swan and Edgar – one immediately wants to know when this happened? For the historically-minded collector this is a tremendously fascinating outlet.

Aide Memoire

Towards the end of the eighteenth century there appeared a great many printed fans which helped young ladies' memories, with dance-steps, words and music of contemporary songs, historical data, rules for card-games and a variety of other serendipities which they would have blushed to have forgotten. For the older lady there were plans of theatre boxes (given out at gala performances, which were fun to keep when one could boast that the Prince Regent, with his guests, sat two tiers below you) or botanical details of flowers of the field (hitherto dismissed as "weeds" but made interesting because of the popularity of Sir Joseph Banks) and maps of either counties of England or countries overseas. These are now surprisingly scarce, for, although cheap in their day, they were thrown away when used or out of date. Prices come between $4-$50.

Alphabet

These are cheap, strong fans with simple lessons for teaching children.

Art Deco

These fans of the 1920's are not always as cheap to produce as earlier fans of the period 1900-1914; they often come in painted gauzes and can be very pretty and feminine. The way one can often recognise them at once is the manner in which they come to a point in the centre of the fan, with sloping sides, which, when folded, produce a zig-zag effect. They can be made of paper, highly coloured, or in textiles with "sweet-pea" colours. They sell around the $10-$30 mark.

Articulated

Another name for this type is *"chasse pot"* and they seem to date towards the latter end of the eighteenth century and some into the nineteenth century. Their purpose is to amuse both the owner and the viewer. They bear all the hallmarks of an ordinary fan of the period, i.e. a total length of about ten inches to 11 inches, with sticks set fairly wide apart to let in the light. On the whole, these sticks are straight, but with some carving, and certainly some other treatment, such as silvering, to make them interesting; the leaves being of good proportion with, possibly, three vignettes of contemporary life upon them, against a delicately painted background. All of this is quite normal: it is when you come to the guards that the secret is revealed.

The guards are fractionally heavier than usual and, at the top, there is a small (generally oval) medallion or portrait. Running alongside the guard is a slim metal rod which, when pushed up and down, makes something happen to that medallion. For instance there is a *chasse pot* fan in the Oldham Collection which has a portrait of a lady of fashion holding a tiny domino in her hand: when activated it shows that the elbow is hinged and she can therefore lift her domino up to cover her face.

These fans are rare and expensive and quite often made by German fan makers; one, sold in 1970 (when fans were relatively cheap) fetched $500.

Assignat

After the holocaust of the French Revolution there was almost total collapse in the monetary system in France and many people paid their bills with "IOU's" or *Assignats* (whose literal meaning was 'to assign to'). As a result fans were made with the decoration covered with these *assignats* and useless bank notes, often having the seven of diamonds melting into the design, just to show that money was hardly worth one tenth of its value after 1794.

Autograph

In Western Europe ordinary people became interested in the autographs of the famous during the latter half of the nineteenth century – writers, musicians and artists. The enormous fans of the time gave ample room for various contemporary celebrities to use one blade each of a large wooden brisé fan and "do their own thing" upon it. It made up a simply fascinating patchwork of the celebrities of the time.

Some only contributed signatures. These chiefly from musicians and people of the stage. But writers could inscribe a line or two and painters really came into their own. Probably the *autograph* fan owned by the Countess of Rosse is the most famous of all with its shaped, double-glazed frame on a turned mahogany stand. These fans are rare and very expensive today.

Balloon

Another name for this wide collection of fans showing early hot-air balloons is *Montgolfières*, and they date from 1783. The first hot-air balloon was invented by Joseph and Etienne Montgolfièr in 1782 and the hydrogen balloon was invented by Professor Charles in 1783.

Fortunately the Montgolfièr brothers were also in the business of making paper and – as paper is essential in the preparation of cheap etched fans, and the ballooning business was taken up so enthusiastically – a great deal of publicity was given to both enterprises simultaneously.

Fans of this type really come under the heading "commemorative" but, as they are both rare and varied, they are listed in catalogues under "ballooning" rather than "etched" or "printed" or even "paper".

Battoir

This type applies to fans with very few sticks (as few as six or eight) which obviously, when folded, lead to extremely wide pleats in the leaf. As a result the guards have to be very wide in order to "guard" the painted leaf; the name *battoir* which means "racquet", shows the shape of the stick.

The people associated with *battoir* fans are the Spanish, but that does not mean to imply that the fans were actually made in Spain. As far as is now known they were made in either Holland or France for the Spanish market. On the whole the leaf was brilliantly coloured and the very few sticks were carved extremely elaborately and then gilded and silvered and sometimes painted to look like enamelwork as well – all to balance up with the extravagant leaf.

They were available in both the eighteenth and nineteenth centuries.

Brazilian

For some reason fans made with humming-birds in the centre have acquired the overall name of *Brazilian* fans. Yet they could have been made in any of the half a dozen South American countries where it is hot and the hummingbird exists. However they can be enchanting.

They are usually made into a complete circle, often of white duck feathers sewn onto a canvas background, built up with fluffy feathers (such as maribou) and then, as a centrepiece, an iridescent hummingbird is placed complete with all its feathers and long, curved, pointed beak.

On occasion there are additions in the way of extra iridescent beetles' wings scattered about the feathers, catching the light.

The fan can be flat on one side, with the decoration on the other, or it can have similar decorations on both sides (which makes putting it down when not in use a problem – it has to be held in a stand.) These fans come in a multitude of colours; a mixture of red and white background feathers or a froth of sugar-pink, palest celestial blue, acid lemon yellow, pistachio green or even a rainbow effect…all with the stuffed hummingbird alighting into the centre.

As the fan did not fold it would have a single rigid handle, made of wood or ivory

and the overall length of these types of fans was about ten to fourteen inches only. There was one in the Preston Exhibition of 1976 ("The World of the Fan", put on as a collaboration between the Fan Circle and the Harris Museum and Art Gallery) which was dated c.1878 and came in shaped box marked "M. Luiza Bittacourt. Florista Rio de Janiero" …showing that this was, in truth, a *Brazilian* fan.

Bridal

Another name is a **Marriage** fan. This type covers a multitude of fans which appear, in their decoration, to have any allusion to the state of marriage e.g. cupids with bows and arrows, putti hovering above the altar of Hymen, true lovers knots, hearts and flowers and so on. In fact they were basically made as a gift from the groom to the bride, would incorporate her initials in the decoration (and sometimes his as well) and would refer to the families in some way.

Smaller and less expensive fans on the same lines would be given to the attendants of the bride and it is known that whole wedding parties have each been given one as a souvenir.

They could be made of whatever was fashionable at the time; e.g. silk, ivory, lace. Dependent upon the quality would be the price today; a French c.1760 *bridal* fan recently fetched $56, some others have gone for as little as $28 and yet others have fetched over $600. They are exclusive, personal, rare and historic but only of real value if they have their entire provenance, showing the names of the parties, the date and the country where the event took place.

Brisé

This is a fan with no leaf, made entirely from rigid or semi-rigid sticks which broaden towards the outside edge and are held in place at the base by a rivet and at the ouside edge by an elaborately threaded ribbon.

There are basically two types: those which are ribboned along the outside edge itself and those which have a slender ribbon which thread through, fairly simply, about an inch down from the outside edge. In both cases the ribbon has to be of a type which has no woven edge, for that becomes too thick when the fan is folded.

The first type is very often varnished or japanned and it is interesting to note how they are made. To begin with the sticks are all made exactly the same; flat, square and broader at the edge, gradually tapering down to a waisted effect, ending with an almond-shaped tip. A small hole is then cut into each tip, through which will go the rivet.

The guards are rarely much larger than each stick, merely thicker. It appears that, in general, the guards are painted all over first, not necessarily with any reference to the design on the stick, but often with reference to the smaller designs in the lower oval (if there is one) of the total fan.

Then the entire fan is ribboned (see Chapter 8), leaving the sticks lying free at the base or rivet end. Some fans of this type are also numbered by the fan maker, like the parts of furniture when being made. After this the fan is painted over with a background colour, on the dark side,

covering three-quarters of the stick; this treatment is carried out on both sides, which could be entirely different. Then the rivet tube is inserted from the back, up through the holes in turn, towards the obverse side, leaving the rivet-screw waiting on one side, so that various sections can be lifted out at will until the whole painting is finished.

From an original finished picture, design is painted onto the flat sticks, working from left to right, with such things as an arm or leg slightly extended on the stick, making sure that the following (covering) stick will close over the top. Thus, should the ribbon not hold it absolutely exactly in place, the design will not appear to "gap" when opened because the precaution has been taken of extending the painting.

No stick is painted right across; it is more likely three-quarters of the way, leaving the remainder plain. When the whole fan is dry, it is turned over and the other side painted. Finally the rivet screw is twirled into its socket, the rose-cut "stone" (real on occasions, otherwise glinting paste) finishing it all off. Fans like these do not have paper "spacers", for they have to fit tightly with no gaps…the spacers are needed more for mother-of-pearl, which can grate against itself.

The rivet tubes are infinitely fine and the greatest care must be used to remove them, possibly the first time they have been really disturbed for up to 250 years, because since extreme age will have made the edge of the tubular section very brittle, it might disintegrate without the support of the screw inside.

If you have to take one apart it is wisest to hold the top of the tube very lightly with a pair of eyebrow tweezers when returning the screw inside, otherwise it will all flake apart.

A painted, wooden, Spanish, late nineteenth *brisé* fan recently fetched $30 in auction with, in the same sale, an ivory, English *brisé* fan of 1795 fetching $394. French japanned fans can go very much higher because of the quality of the painting rather than the material used.

Broken

Three names all mean virtually the same in this case: **broken, puzzle** or **trick**. It is all a question of the way the fan has been ribboned; for the whole idea is to embarass your friend when allowing him or her to spread out your fan. Opened normally it will exhibit some innocuous scene – that is, opening it up from left to right. But you would suggest to your friend that there is another scene if opened from right to left; the moment they attempt to do this the whole fan appears to fall apart. In fact the ribboning is carried out in such a way that two ribbons are used all through and the sticks of the *brisé* fan are actually finished off in six or eight completely separate sections.

The effect is unnerving, to say the least. But the owner can just gather up the apparently fractured fan and open it again in the normal way and it is "mended" again.

There is another type of *puzzle* fan which is also very clever, again of a *brisé* formation. Open it up from left to right and you see a complete picture, but you realise that the sticks happen to be very close together, overlapping by half on each occasion. Then, still on the obverse side, open it up from right to left and there is quite another scene. Turn it over and repeat the process on the reverse and, in the end, you have found a fan with no less than four completely different pictures. In the East it is well-known that the fourth side might even produce a hilariously funny pornographic scene. These last are sometimes referred to as "double-entendre" fans.

Cabriolet

These fans are rare, great fun to look at because of the many details, and can be dated from 1755...most being made between 1755–65. The invention of a cabriolet (a light, two-wheeled, one-horse chaise, with fewer spokes to the wheels than hitherto used) by Josiah Childs in 1755 had the frivolous world in a twirl with excitement. Everything was immediately decorated in the same way – waistcoats, stockings, caps etc – and fans followed suit. Now the fan would have fewer sticks and either two leaves or mounts across them, showing the sticks stretching up in between. Miss Esther Oldham's Collection, now in the Museum of Fine Arts in Boston, has several *cabriolet* fans of note.

Firstly there is an extremely rare *mourning cabriolet* which must be one of a kind; it is painted in grisaille, with ivory sticks carved with the initials of the deceased in between the two paper leavers. Another, of the same date, c.1755, shows a most curious Chinoiserie *cabriolet* made of vellum, where the upper section, which should show the sticks has, instead, an area of découpé work. The rest of the fan is delightfully painted with Chinoiserie scenes. A third most unusual *cabriolet* in the same collection is a triple one; i.e. having three painted vellum leaves altogether, and smothered in a riot of enchanting vignettes, painted in all those porcelain colours of the period.

If you can buy a cabriolet fan it is always wise to try and get one which actually shows little ladies of fashion riding about in their "cabs". The price would start at about $350 and soar upwards.

Camaieu

A painting on a fan-leaf of different shades of the same colour, mostly rose or blue, camaieu was popular in the eighteenth century. *Grisaille* means the same technique, but always in tones of grey.

Caricature

Generally fans like these are dual-national; for instance there was a *caricature* fan recently for sale with a paper leaf, painted on both sides with scenes of social life, profusely inscribed with both French and German observations, c.1780...and which sold for $10. Others have been known which fetched as much as $150.

Celluloid

Some sticks for fans have always been made of a celluloidal composition from Regency days to the advertising fans of the 1930s. Over the years the composition of celluloid has altered considerably, but basically it is a "solid inflammable material consisting essentially of soluble cellulose nitrate and camphor". It can be transparent (imitating tortoiseshell) or opaque (imitating ivory) and it can come in any colour.

To make black celluloid one dips into a solution of nitrate of silver; for yellow, one first immerses in a solution of nitrate of lead, then in a concentrated solution of chromate of potash; for brown, one dips into a solution of permanganate of potash made strongly alkaline by the addition of soda, and so on.

If the celluloid has become discoloured superficially, you can wipe it with a woollen rag wetted with absolute alcohol and ether mixed in equal proportions; this dissolves and removes a minute superficial layer and lays bare a new surface. To restore the polished appearance you should rub briskly first with a woollen cloth and finish with silk or fine chamois with a spot of jeweller's rouge. Celluloid dissolves in acetone, sulphuric ether, alcohol, oil of turpentine and benzine. It can also be softened in hot water, and in steam (120ºC, 248ºF): it becomes so soft it can be kneaded like dough. Its greatest liability is that it is so inflammable.

Celluloid was often used in the past for cheap fan sticks but they need quite a bit of care when cleaning or mending them today. An adhesive for celluloid is made from 2 parts of shellac, 3 parts of spirit of camphor and 4 parts of strong alcohol dissolved in a warm place. This glue must be kept well corked-up.

If a fan has celluloid sticks which have broken they can be mended by the above method and then painted upon with gouache colours and/or gilding agents. But always be careful of a naked flame.

Chapel

The *chapel* fan was first published in 1796, years after the first church fans; and the ones used in chapel services give printed prayers and psalms but there is never a mention of praying for the Royal Family.

Children

The alphabet fan has already been mentioned, but *children's* fans go a little further, not only being educational, but beautifully painted like the fans owned by their mothers, but in miniature. They were made from chicken-skin, vellum, paper or silk and are very much in demand today.

Church

The first of the church fans appeared in England during the 1720's. They gave prayers, the Ten Commandments, the Creed and special prayers for the Royal Family. In America *church* fans were available as you went in through the door of the church, made from turkey feathers or palmetto leaves, together with prayer-books and hymnals. A *church* or *chapel* fan would fetch in the region of $40 today – made from paper with wooden sticks.

Cockade

This is a pleated fan opening out into a complete circle, the end-sticks forming a long double handle. Very often the leaf was made from satin, but vellum and silk, as well as paper, have been used.

Commemorative

See **Printed**.

Découpé

This means something which has a cut and pierced leaf which can be made of vellum, chicken-skin or either silvered or gilded hand-made paper. It gives a beautiful effect to look like patterned netting or the earliest forms of lace, such as sixteenth century reticella. This effect is carried out with tiny little scissors or surgical knives. The earliest examples are the one known to have been in the Cluny Museum, possibly owned by Henri III, and the other owned by Miss Esther Oldham, now in Boston. Miss Oldham's fan also has insertions of mica, to give it added texturing, but does not come up into architectural "points" like the one at Cluny.

Découpé fans existed from the sixteenth to the eighteenth centuries, and some in the eighteenth century were prettily overlaid with gilding, the découpé-work being as fine as a pricked design for laces. In fact, the designs themselves can be so similar that it would be interesting to discover whether there were pattern-books to which makers could refer.

Fans of the eighteenth century are nowadays sold for around $70-$150. There are no *découpé* fans left of the sixteenth century (they all seem to exist in the contemporary paintings) and those of the seventeenth century are rare.

Domino

A fan which can either be plain or covered all over with a painted design and in which, often asymetrically placed, are cut two holes for one's eyes to peer through is known as a domino. There is another type, with a painted mask upon it, which is named a **Mask** fan. In both cases it was supposed that a lady might attend a risqué play or gathering without giving away her identity; of course it did nothing of the sort but it did, at least, pay lip-service to convention. A fan of this type would start at about $100 and rise rapidly; dependent upon its decoration, condition and age.

Empire

This period (1804–1815) derives its name from the era during which Napoleon reigned as Emperor, and under his rule warmer fabrics came into fashion and taffetas, velvets and brocades were again in vogue; classical white still predominating as the main colour.

However, no-one was prepared to forget the effects of the Revolution in a hurry, so fashions for fans no longer affected diamond-encrusted coronets on the guards or even elaborate paintings on vellum.

Change was in the air, so fans changed, too. They were small, to suit the skirts which no longer were draped over crinolines, small enough to be called "Lilliputians" or even "Imperceptibles"; and they were made of far less costly materials than seen in the Georgian age.

Horn and bone predominated for the sticks, some with cut-steel piqué-work on them, and there was a great deal of plain, smooth wood. The leaves were of net, some

spangled and sequined, or silk, gauzes or satin. Gradually the colour began to alter, deepening in tone, but the flavour throughout was of a cheaper fan, made all-of-a-piece, to contrast with the clothes and to catch the attention with little flashes of light sparking off the spangles.

Feather

On the whole people associate feather fans with ostrich feathers during the graceful Edwardian age. Fans both rigid or folding have, in fact, been made of every type of feather imaginable from the beginning of time. And some of these feathers are virtually unknown to us today.

Some fans have feathers placed individually into a design, for instance to enhance the painted plumage of a bird, and the majority of these were created by Dutch or German fan makers. But the fans made entirely from feathers most commonly found nowadays are those made with peacock, pheasant or ostrich feathers.

The female ostrich has all-brown feathers or white feathers edged with brown: the male owns the all-white feathers. They are extremely easy to dye (see chapter 8) and equally easy to clean and re-curl. Where one has to take great care is in handling them when carrying them home from the saleroom. Generally the new owner wishes to cover the feathers with some protective material – but this is more than liable to break the spines of old plumes. It is best to place the whole fan in tissue-paper and hold it with the feathers hanging downwards, the handle uppermost, until the fan is safely home and can be dealt with as necessary. This is especially important if the feather fan has a mere one or two feathers, as in the 1930's. The price would vary from $10-$100, dependent more on the material of the sticks.

Top left. *An envelope entitled "The Cremorne Rose", the accompanying "rose" fan unopened, and the fan completely opened to show various views of items in the Gardens – which were places to visit, like those at Ranelagh and Vauxhall. Printed by C. Adleis printing establishment, Hamburg, and published by Joseph Meyers and Co., 144 Leadenhall Street, London. 1855. Shown together with a contemporary Christmas card which, when the top ribbon is pulled, opens up to form a small fan.*
Centre left. *An advertising fan for the Café Martin, New York on the obverse and, on the reverse "Perfumed with Pompeia, L.T. Piver, Paris, France". The date is uncertain, as is the reason for the aeroplanes.*
Bottom left. *Viennese fan. c. 1890, showing a silk leaf painted with four dogs' heads. The wooden sticks are painted to simulate a striated wood and one guard is studded with a fine miniature of a dog's head under an Essex crystal.*
Top right. *A mock rococo English fan, delicately painted on silk. The sticks are of bone, impressed with some gilding. c. 1905.*
Right. *The fan leaf is painted to show a military encampment, the ivory sticks pierced and painted, folding to form bundles of rods caught by bands, one pierced with a heart. Probably Dutch. c. 1780.*

early one was known to belong to Marie Antoinette (she was sadly short-sighted) and the fashion continued through into the nineteenth century. In general the fan was perfectly normal for the prevailing fashion but, somewhere in its construction, there would be placed a form of magnifiying-glass. The best place was within the sticks or guard – and this, elegantly used, was the fashionable lady's answer to a man's monocle.

Man's

It is well-known that gentlemen carried fans during the eighteenth century; what is more difficult is to distinguish how they differed from the lady's fan. It has been suggested that the way one can tell is to search for a "bug" on the decoration of a fan. Apparently that, or a beetle or a mosquito on the painted scene of a fan shows it belonged to a man. Certainly one gathers that a man's fan was larger than a lady's but, as so many men could be so overtly effeminate during that time, and often men gave friends gifts of fans, it also follows that men had similar fans to ladies.

Minuet

This is slightly problematical as a name for a fan, for it is a name which now is all-embracing and no one precise definition will find total agreement amongst experts.

I consider that a minuet fan is a brisé fan, made from ivory, bone, wood or horn, sometimes with a sprinkling of piqué-work upon it, sometimes with painted garlands of flowers, but almost always smallish and making an attempt to create a filigree effect in the chosen material. I feel they should be dated from c.1810 onwards, growing slightly larger as the years went by, and out of fashion by the 1850's. They fetch from $20 upwards.

Filigree

The best filigree is made in China, Norway, Malta, Spain or Portugal. Filigree fans are really rather pointless as they allow the virtually unrestricted passage of air, but they can be rather beautiful. Silver or gold filigree was generally used for the sticks or guards, with a fairly heavy leaf set above to counteract the weight problem. Some interesting Portugese filigree fans were made for use in Brazil, and filigree, as a whole, was generally gilded in order to prevent the silver tarnishing. It was also a method in which enamels might be used, to spark up the overall effect with colour rather than using more costly gemstones. There are very fine examples in both the Messel and the Oldham collections, but, on the whole, they are relatively rare.

Gauze

Many a Victorian fan was made of gauze, painted with scenes of anything from putti playing in clouds to a pseudo-Watteau effect. Generally there were additions of lace borders and insertions, the sticks were of horn, wood, some blonde tortoiseshell or bone, and they sell from $20 upwards.

Lace

The subject has been dealt with more fully in chapter four, but suffice to say that some perfectly lovely lace fans were available during the nineteenth century which had ivory or shaded mother-of-pearl sticks. Recently an example, c.1870 was sold for $30 and another for $80…everything depends upon the quality of the article.

Lorgnette

There is a purely practical aspect to this fan, which can also be very pretty indeed – that of being able to see through a spy-glass. An

Mourning

In the eighteenth century mourning fans were carried in place of colourful and frivolous fashionable fans; they were generally "en grisaille" and classical in subject matter. In the nineteenth century ladies could carry a fan which was stark black as a sign of their deep sorrow. A well-painted Georgian fan recently fetched $120 in a sale. Plain black comes cheaper – but it is rare to find a mourning fan in mint condition, they were well used over the years.

Neapolitan

The tourist trade to Rome and Naples from the seventeenth century onwards inspired a great many fans made in Naples or showing scenes about Naples and the surrounding country, notably Vesuvius. Most are made at the turn of the century into 1800, some earlier and some later. They are neo-classical in essence, some are perfectly beautifully painted on chicken-skin and some are obviously "dashed off" on paper. In recent sales they have fetched between $120–$640.

Panorama

There was every attempt to amuse the owner as well as the onlooker when fans became a normal part of every lady's dress; one way being with a fan which gave you a foretaste of the cinema. The fan was fixed and had a small handle at one side. Turning the handle produced a series of pictures which could be seen in the centre of the fan. The pictures were actually in a long continuous strip, being wound over two rolls of wood or ivory at the back, and could be sent either forwards or backwards. One famous type showed views of the Gardens of Versailles. This type is difficult to find nowadays.

Paper

Until 1840 almost all paper used for fans was made by hand, therefore being much stronger and more resilient than cheap paper of the late nineteenth century. Paper was used for fans when they were to be printed, etched, lithographed and so on. There are a multitude of types, for they are sub-divided into "advertising", "political" etc. In most cases they had cheap wooden sticks and the paper leaf was a "thing of the moment", the leaf being stripped off and replaced by another the moment the news changed. (This was the origin of "off with the old, on with the new!") "The Oracle" fan recently fetched $76 and a Commemorative one $92.

Sandalwood

If you wished to make ice-cream in India before the advent of the refrigerator, you placed your mixture in a covered bowl, hung it in a gunny-sack from a tree in the full glare of the sun and poured water over it. Then you set a small boy to swing the sack in the sunshine, back and forth, continuing to pour tepid water over it. In no time you had ice-cream.

Sandalwood fans work in the same way. You sit in the shade, continually dipping your sandalwood fan in a bowl of tepid water and then waving it in front of your face. It makes an icy breeze and smells wonderfully aromatic.

Some fans made from this smooth, easy-to-carve wood have been painted or covered with cut-steel piqué; this is really a pity because then you dare not dip them in the water first. There is no limit to the period in which sandalwood fans have been made, for they are still being made today. Those for sale in Europe have usually been made in countries such as Burma, Malaya etc and then decorated in France or England. Prices have varied from $6 to $160.

Telescope

These are convenience fans which can be folded up and put away in the small reticules used by ladies in the nineteenth century when it was no longer fashionable nor desirable to have your page walk behind you, carrying all your belongings.

The fan itself can be made in several ways, but the main effect is that the leaf or mount is small in comparison to the length of the sticks, which are hinged and fold in half. It is also possible to have a fan in which the leaf rests in the normal way upon the sticks but, when gently pushed up, extends upwards with further sticks concealed inside, doubling the length of the fan. When concertinaed back into place the sticks go inside the leaf and the lower section of the guards fit snugly into the broader, upper section.

There is another type known as a "parasol" fan which can be fixed onto some projection in your carriage, loosened at a hinge in order to bend the parasol-fan to shade your face and then used as a fan in the normal way. A recent eighteenth century example, probably Russian, fetched $76 in a sale.

Many other fans exist which include many other shapes and materials too. But they have either been written about in other books or they are simply not collectible today. Prices see-saw, which is great fun because it means everyone has an opportunity to buy a surprise now and then. But no-one should ever buy a fan without first looking hard at the fans offered for sale. One can read too much into catalogue entries and some sound glorious, but are not quite to one's taste when seen – and others, sold in a lot, might be just right to start a collection.

The more sales you attend (without buying) the more you can begin to recognise known collectors' and dealers' faces around you. Sometimes they might have to buy two fans in a lot, wanting only one of them, and you may be able to manage a private sale on the side afterwards. Equally, as time goes by, you begin to recognise old favourites coming up again. Very few people can really afford to collect indiscriminately, splashing money about; so, when a change is due, fans get turned out by collectors and they go for something more exciting or rarified, and you can slip in and pick up their discards.

It is not something of which to be ashamed: nowadays one needs all the help possible over provenance and it greatly enhances your fan if it is known to have featured in some famous collection in the past.

Oriental Fans

It is pointless to expect Oriental fans to resemble European fans because the world-wide use of the fan began in the earliest times and was, in effect, a statement of the philosophy of each individual culture regarding the use of regalia and social stature.

Of course everyone picked up large leaves and fanned themselves when they were hot – every soul in every hot country! But then, in order to show the importance of a ruler his clothes and possessions had to be richer than his vassals and had to be seen to be more impressive. On approaching a group, sitting under the shade of a Bò-tree on a sweat-running day, what would be the first thing one would notice amongst the loin-clothed men? The central man's more important-looking fan.

Time has gone by, civilisations have altered, philosophies have been embroidered with cant but men and women remain the same...hot in the Summer and needing to cool down with a fan or an air-conditioning unit in order to be comfortable. That is a totally basic relief to any hot person in any hot country, East or West.

Several books on the history of the fan have recently been written, so it is space-wasting to give the background here in the same way. However, very little has been written about the different attitudes of the Chinese and the Japanese to the art of fan-painting – a completely different philosophy from that of the Western world. Let me recount a fairly well-known tale:

According to a popular Chinese legend, the Universe at the beginning of time was one enormous egg.

One day the egg split open, the upper half became the sky, the lower half became the earth...and from the earth emerged primordial man. Every day this man grew ten feet taller, the sky grew ten feet higher and the earth grew ten feet thicker.

After eighteen thousand years this first man died. His head split apart and became the Sun and the Moon, while his blood filled the rivers and the seas. His hair became the forests and the meadows, his perspiration became the rain, his breath became the wind, his voice became the thunder – and his fleas became our ancestors!

A people's idea of its origins generally gives a clue as to what they think is most important in life and this legend expresses a typically Chinese view-point; in other words they feel that man is *not* the culminating achievement of the creation, but that man is a relatively insignificant part in the scheme of life – hardly more than an afterthought in fact. Nature, its beauty, splendour and bounty, comes first.

This story is in direct contrast to the Western world, where, after the birth of Christ, a philosophy was preached in which man should love his fellow-man. In the East this concept of "love" is unknown and "discipline and duty" are one's aims. Certainly the concept, held by Christians, that God created man in His own image is both terrifying and absurd in the East, where they believe in their personal unworthiness in the presence of Nature; their object being an attempt to find in Nature a niche from which they might contemplate the grandeur of all things created.

It is in this deep humility that we must seek the key to the arts of the people. They have a great reverence for a mystery (are not the ways of Nature mysterious? Who can predict a horrendous earthquake, a famine-spreading drought or fierce winds in those pitiless climates?) and it is through this world of semi-knowledge that the Chinese have sought and found their artistic inspiration. They manipulate the cult of the vague, contriving to give the impression of a completeness more complete than anything else that can be defined in human terms. The Chinese artist's mystery is of this earth, reflecting the seasons and humours, giving an atmosphere to what man can see in his immediate surroundings and revealing, in a sudden flash of knowledge, man's harmony with Nature.

What is important to remember is that, in ideal circumstances, the Chinese artist would never sell his works to anyone. Poetry, calligraphy and paintings – the three sublime arts – are practised by the learned for the benefit of the learned, sometimes for the sole enjoyment of the artist himself. These *literati* explore the depths of their knowledge for their own enjoyment, filling their works with allusions and quotations which they alone are capable of understanding; it is for this reason that Chinese art demands from the spectator more co-operation than the art of any other nation. The ignorant are dismissed, their works are for interpretive eyes and souls alone, delicately embracing only a favoured few.

No wonder it is difficult for the people of the Western world to understand even one remote section of Oriental art and its background philosophies! We have none of their background knowledge, we cannot read their beautiful calligraphy, we cannot appreciate their philosophical viewpoints unless, for some long time, we have lived amongst them and have had a sympathetic teacher. All we can really do is to try and appreciate the curving flow of a brush-stroke, the contrasts of colour-tones, the positioning of a poem and study aspects of their own insight into Nature.

Chinese and Japanese painted fans, whatever their shape, are considered as artistic paintings; fans from the Western world are considered as amalgams of the crafts. Naturally there are times when an Oriental fan has intricate sticks which are pure craft and there are some very fine paintings on European fans, but, in the main, one should consider Chinese and Japenese fans as primarily "paintings". (The word "art" is too nebulous, meaning "skill as the result of knowledge and practice".)

As Chinese fan paintings were created for the élite and the enlightened *by* the élite and the enlightened (and never by the mere artisan) so no nation has produced more (non-scientific) literature on art than the Chinese, the training-ground of the would-be scholar.

Chinese scholars used brushes for their writing, writing which emerged as a simplified form from original small sketches of objects. The duty of the Chinese artist is also to represent objects through emotions (wonder, fear and so on). From a harmonious spirit (the only way in which one can co-ordinate the mind and the hand) the artist has to attune himself to total serenity in order to render his subject with a rythmic background realisation of the equilibriums of all life within Nature, the continuous succession of the seasons and the balance of good and evil. Then he makes that fateful decision to paint a certain aspect of a subject …it might take months of thought before real inspiration floats upon his spirit.

He cannot afford to make a mistake; there is no rubbing out, for the materials the artist chooses to use, either silk or paper, may be centuries old and are slightly absorbent. Therefore his marks will be indelible. So it is quite possible that many preliminary sketches will be made and gradually fined down until the mere *essence* of a statement is arrived at. "They create a pool for those who are able to swim in it". Then the original sketches are burned as being unworthy.

As painting is derived from calligraphy one "reads" a painting like a book or a poem, starting at the top and gradually descending. The seal or accompanying poem is often placed at the top for the same reason. On the other hand landscapes are viewed as though standing out in the countryside, unable to see all about unless one turns one's head in a sweeping arc. So you "read" a landscape from one side to another.

In Europe it is often a sneer to say that a painter has copied another's style or composition. In the East the reverse is true. Out of their humility many great artists deliberately work in the style of some former or greater artist as the truest compliment they could pay him, and this attitude is much admired, for it also imposes a higher sense of self-discipline and negates too free .an expression.

For instance there is the tradition named after Wen T'ung (1018–1079) who was Governor of the Hu-chou district. He was a member of a very select group of *literati* aesthetes and the first really great painter of bamboos, hence his name was frequently invoked by later painters of this subject.

I am indebted to Mr Milne Henderson (99 Mount Street, London W.l.) for permission to quote from his catalogue: *"The Art of Chinese Fan Painting",* and for the especially good introduction by Mr John Hay, Lecturer in East Asian Art at the School of Oriental and African Art, University of London. I quote it in full, for several new facets reveal themselves about fans from the East, not heretofore mentioned in books on the subject. For those who are unable to come to Mr and Mrs Henderson's gallery the facts mentioned by Mr John Hay make the many fan paintings more comprehensible.

"The Chinese fan holds a double pleasure for the Westerner today. To begin with, there is the peculiar fascination of rediscovering an object that once was so everyday in its own culture that acquaintance with its usage and associated customs seems to bring to life a whole society. Secondly there is the fact that the fan, which in Europe was little more than a fancy appendage for fashionable gentlewomen, in China was often a vehicle for the fine arts. For the Chinese fan was ubiquitous, and invariably decorated, and the hands of the greatest artists of their age were often turned to this purpose.

"In traditional China down to the present century, the variety of fans was prolific, almost every district and every social group having its peculiar type. "Banana fans" were made from a variety of large leaves. Woven fans, often of extreme fineness, used rushes, grain-stalks and slivers of bamboo. "Jade-plaque" fans were elegantly carved from solid sheets of the giant bamboo from Chekiang province. Often decorated material was pasted on the face of the fan or stretched over a frame. The "duck's-foot fan" from Kuangtung province was made from a continuous length of bamboo, with half its length split into radiating spokes, over which paper was stretched. It was well-known to Westerners in the late nineteenth century and they called it the Swatow fan, since its decoration was often done in that town.

"A fan of particular interest for its sociology was the 'oiled fan' from Hangchou. This was a folding fan made from black, oiled persimmon-bark paper and decorated with gold splashes. In the mid-nineteenth century its use was confined to labourers, since black was symbolic of moral defilement. But towards the end of the century its popularity began a rapid, unexplained rise through the social ranks, until it became fashionable with even the aristocracy and examples of it, delicately painted with gold and silver pictures, were the cutomary present to provincial officials leaving to take up office in the capital.

"Different designs of fans varied in their efficiency and this brought about set habits of usage. The ubiquitous importance of the fan in the Far East was due to the cooling air it wafted, so it was a social gaffe to produce a fan before society considered it justified by the weather. At the onset of summer, on a certain day dictated by fashion, the land would blossom with fans. At first, folding fans were *de rigeur.* In the second month of summer, the stretched-fan was produced, while the ultimate feather-fan was properly reserved for the dog-days of the third month. While fans were in use, they were put to other advantages. Ranking officials borne in sedan-chairs through the streets, when so meeting each other were permitted to cover their faces with a fan. This avoided elaborate and time-consuming rituals. A term for fans commonly found in twelfth and thirteenth century texts, *pien-mien,* meaning 'to convenience the fact', reflects a long history to this custom.

"The fan of silk stretched over a circumferential frame and the fan of paper stretched over folding ribs are today the best known of all types. Round fans on long handles are commonly illustrated in stone-engraved pictures of the second century AD and later. There is a very famous tale of a concubine of the Emperor Ch'eng-ti (r.32–36 BC) who fell from favour and consequently wrote a poem on a round fan, which she then sent in to the Emperor. In the poem she compared herself to the fan, shining and full as the moon when the weather was warm,

but gathering dust on the shelf when autumn came. Ever since then, the term "Autumn fan" has meant a lady whose charms have wilted.

"The stretched silk fan was for many centuries the principal cooling device of the Chinese. Its early association with writing is amusingly illustrated by another tale, about the great scholar and calligrapher, Wang Hsi-chih. Wang, who was very famous in his own time and subsequently became known as the patriarchal "sage of calligraphy", once passed an old woman selling fans by the road side. He took them off her, quickly wrote a few lines upon each and handed them back. The woman was incensed at this despoilation of her stock, but later amazed when it sold out within minutes.

"The practice of decorating fans must have become widespread and by the twelfth century this is very well attested. The emperor Hui-tsung (r.1101–1126) enthusiastically promoted a court academy of the arts and was himself a highly accomplished artist. Whenever he decorated a fan, this immediately set a fashion.

"The art of the following two centuries (Southern Sung dynasty, 1127–1279) is typically that of the court and among its most distinctive concerns was the writing of elegant inscriptions and the painting of exquisitely selected morsels of Nature on stretched fans. Examples survive from the hands of emperors and empresses. Fans of this design are, indeed, sometimes called

Top left. *Three telescopic Victorian fans showing how the fan is lengthened by pulling the leaf up from the sticks to almost double their length. Possibly Spanish.*

Centre left. *Early Georgian fan. The leaf is painted with scenes representing Alexander and the family of Darius, the reverse the disclosing of Achilles' subterfuge. The ivory sticks are carved and pierced, with portraits of King George II and six members of the Royal Family, a lion and a unicorn, with silver piqué, reading "The Royal Family". English.*

Bottom left. *Two fine handscreens. c. 1860. English, with beadwork in opalescent beads, pure silk fringe and ribbons, with turned wood handles part painted gold.*

Below. *Children's and dolls' fans. Group of five tiny fans, including an 'aide memoire' of ivory, complete with pencil. The others are made from spangles on gauze, pierced sandalwood, painted vellum and a japanned brisé fan. 19th century.*

"palace fans". Usually they are round, but can also be six-cornered, gourd-shaped and pear-shaped. The silk was stretched over an outside frame of very thin wood, which was usually braced by a handle that continued across its diameter behind the silk. The best handles were made from the speckled bamboo, known as "Lady Hsiang", from the central lakes of Hunan province. Lacquered wood and ivory could also be used, but the very elaborate versions made in Canton during the Ch'ing dynasty (1644–1911) were exclusively for the foreign market. The most common Chinese term for this kind of fan is *t'uan-shan* and in Japan, where it was also popular, it is called *uchiwa*.

"The folding fan seems to have been a Japanese invention (in the seventh century AD). It was certainly made in both Japan and Korea by the 11th century and examples brought from there were admired for their ingenuity and beauty by Chinese of that time. They were often painted with pictures, especially of *genre* subjects. Huang T'ing-chien, one of the most famous Chinese scholars and artists of the eleventh century, was presented with a Korean fan and wrote a poem about how it showed him more of that

country than did all the writings of travellers.

"It was apparently not until the beginning of the fifteenth century that the Chinese became sufficiently impressed to copy the Japanese and Korean fans. In this period, a considerable number of diplomatic and trade missions came to China from Japan and the emperor Chèng-tsu (r.1403–1425) was so intrigued by the convenience of the folding fan that he ordered his craftsmen to copy

Above. *An autograph fan with very personal signatures. Horn sticks with cut-steels piqué and an amber-coloured paste rivet. Made in Vienna c. 1903-6.*
Left. *Decoupé or Punched-work fan, early 18th century, the leaf decoupé and punched, gilt, and painted with flowers. Pierced ivory sticks and guard.*
Below. *Cabriolet fan of painted silk gauze, the bone sticks carved in the Philippines for the Spanish market, gilded and silvered. c. 1830. Spanish or French.*

them. So the tradition goes, but another dimension is suggested by the fact that the folding fan became fashionable among the prostitutes, whose society flourished in the sophisticated cities of the south-east, such as Nanking, Hangchou and Shanghai. Ning-po, the port near Shanghai, was where the Japanese ships landed. Such circles, extensively patronised by the wealthy and the educated, were often in the lead of fashion. The folding fan, which could be stowed in the sleeve – or in the high boot of the Chinese gentleman – was the perfect vehicle for inscribed and painted expressions of elegant affection. The ladies of the pleasure quarters were often highly cultured and in the seventeenth century, before Manchu puritanism smothered them, their artistic efforts were collected by some connoisseurs. Such collections were mainly of fan paintings.

"The popularity of the folding fan was,

however, both wide and respectable by the sixteenth century. Since then, they have been the most frequent gift of greeting and farewell, of esteem and congratulation and simply of good feeling at congenial gatherings. They are faced with paper on both sides, so a single fan may bear an extensive message and often refers quite specifically to a valued relationship or treasured moment. Many fans, of course, bear simply a respectful dedication and this generally results from an artist being requested to decorate someone's fan. It would have been quite unacceptable to cool oneself with an implement not thus graced. These inscriptions and paintings reflect educated society much more completely than they could have done in Europe, for the

Top left. *18th century fan, the paper leaf showing a hand-coloured etching in tones of blue. Three amorini and two personages are pictured in a romantic mythical landscape. The ivory sticks are pierced and painted in tones of blue with ribbons and garlands of flowers.*

Centre left. *Empire fan. Made of net and sewn with sequins and spangles; ivory sticks and mother-of-pearl guards, both with cut steels. The central vignette is painted on silk and applied onto the net. Possibly Spanish. c. 1820. From M. Duvelleroy's personal collection.*

Below. *Edwardian fan; double gauze mount enhanced by lace insets and painted with small birds. Plain ivory sticks and guards.*

Top right. *Ballooning fan. The central vignette shows a pastoral scene; the other two views show the ascent of Charles and Robert from the Tuileries on 1st December 1783 – the first proper ascent in a hydrogen balloon. The sticks are of gilded and silvered carved ivory, the guards also have balloon motifs.*

Bottom right. *Spanish fan showing three scenes on vellum, painted in gouache. The battoir shapes of the sticks are typical of the period. Paste rivet. c. 1840-60.*

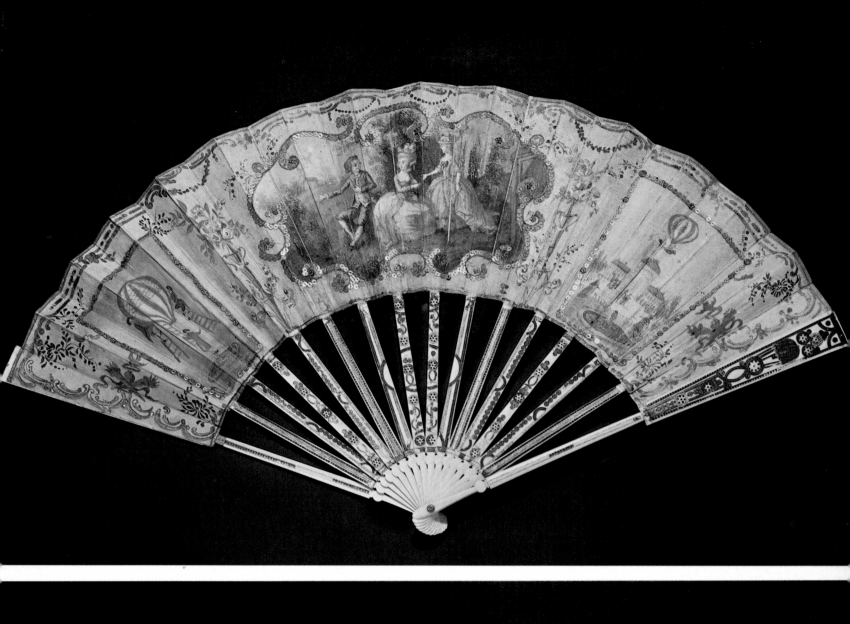

arts of both calligraphy and painting were even more generally practised in China, with her intensely cultivated ideal of the amateur.

"These fans have survived in some numbers precisely because they were often valued more for their artistic than their practical value. Owners sometimes removed the papers from the skeleton and had them mounted as album leaves, retaining to varying extent their signs of wear. In the nineteenth century several fans were sometimes mounted on a wall-scroll. It must be remembered that the Chinese considered calligraphy to be an art even nobler than painting, so that an inscription from a talented hand was treasured correspondingly. Where mounted fans, either from a stretched or a folding original, have passed through Chinese collections, they may have been impressed with personal seals of the collector as well as of the artist.

"Fan paintings have never been considered as seriously as scroll paintings. The Chinese were very hierarchical in their grading of arts according to seriousness of purpose, expressed through orthodoxy of format. But the casual and often self-revealing nature of the fan painting is, conversely, its greatest attraction. The peculiar restrictions of the fan's shape was a challenge to the alert artist and when their compositional solutions turn the difficulties to positive account the results can be striking in the extreme. This is particularly true of the seventeenth and eighteenth centuries, when there was much very original experimentations in these matters.

"The artistic content varied according to purpose, of. course. Some varieties were essentially practical, such as the street-map fans. Neither were many pretensions shown by the current-event fans, such as the gruesome illustrations of the Tientsin massacre in 1870, which sold so rapidly throughout the empire that the government prohibited them. Between the extremes appeared the ingenious dirty-picture fan, which, when opened in the normal manner from left to right, displayed an innocuous flower, but produced startling revelations when opened from right to left. Most pretentious of all was the steel-ribbed fan, introduced from Japan. Its decoration concealed a most effective weapon.

"The earliest painted folding fan surviving, a Japanese example of the late twelfth century, has thirty-four separate wooden leaves. Subsequently, these leaves – or bones, as the Chinese call them – were reduced to a framework and the interstices filled by a silk or paper covering. In the Chinese folding fan, the average number of bones is sixteen and these are known as "large-boned fans". "Small-boned fans" commonly have around twenty-four bones. But there could be from under ten to over thirty bones and the black fans of Hangchou, mentioned earlier, had as many as fifty, opening out to a full semi-circle. Except in such special varieties, folding fans were generally covered with alum-sized paper – giving a distinctively silver gleam – or with gold-decorated coloured paper. This latter was used on congratulatory occasions, such as birthdays and the New Year. The commonest variety is a near-scarlet with liberal gold splotches.

Superior to this is the variety with a much finer sprinkling of gold. The most elegant variety is a waxed red paper that is printed with gold designs. A variation on this is the use of gold "ink" for actually painting on a coloured paper. In China the folding fan is called the *che-shan*. In Japan it is the *ogi*."

Akome-ogi: these are early Far Eastern court fans which were used from the seventh century to the end of the Tokugawa Sh-gunate (1867). They have thirty-eight or thirty-nine blades of wood painted white and decorated with proscribed flower paintings on a ground of gold or silver powder, ornamented at the corners with arrangements of artificial flowers in silk, with twelve long streamers of different coloured silks, the rivet being either a bird or a butterfly.

Akoya-ogi: the Empress of Japan's fans, according to Mary Gostelow, who continues: "it is said that they were decorated with the sacred flowers of the chrysanthemum, plum, pine-tree or orange-blossom."

Cantonese: see "mandarin".

Chauri: an Indian fly-whisk.

Gumbai-uchiwa: These are flat Japanese battle fans, generally made from iron (often beautifully damascened), lacquered wood or hardened leather. The handle, which strengthened the leaf from one end to the next, was of iron and generally covered with leather (for a firmer hold) and had a long cord and tassel, so the fan might be wound round a part of the saddle when not in use. There was an elaborate procedure, when in battle, of signals by the battle commander, with his fan; the obverse usually had his family symbol painted brilliantly in colour, the reverse (according to Mary Gostelow) with a *tomoye* or Buddhist cross – and, dependent upon the way the fan was seen by his troops, so the army would surge forward or retreat.

Gun-sen: a folding or pleated Japanese battle-fan, generally made of toughened leather, with heavy iron guards. When shut this is an extremely effective weapon, for the iron was sharpened into a cutting edge. These fans were made for use between the twelfth to twentieth centuries.

Gyoji-uchiwa: small fans for the use of Japanese referees for wrestling-bouts.

Handscreen: Korea and Japan received this idea from China, according to tradition, at the end of the sixth century; these fans do not pleat or fold and can be made in a multitude of different ways.

Hi-ogi: Mary Gostelow writes that this type of fan could only be used by the Emperor of Japan. It usually had twenty-three sticks of *hinoki* (cyprus wood), prized for its pleasant odour and smooth grain. The fan had a pivot of paper-string, and the outer guard-sticks were each supposed to have had four-foot long (121.9 cm) silk cords formed of seven different colours to symbolise the virtues of the Orient, tied to the sticks with a complicated knot. It appears that this fan was always kept closed, the sticks held in place by a ribbon of white silk.

Jin sen: a Camp fan, from China and Japan, made from the seventh century, created with feathers – such as the pheasant or peacock. The handle was generally lacquered and it was suspended from the girdle by a gold or silver chain.

Kanasawa: these are special fans made for men during the nineteenth century, highly prized, and made in the city of Kanasawa on the West coast of Japan.

Kyoto: these fans were made in Kyoto and etched, for Kyoto was the centre of the art of copper-plate engraving during the whole of the nineteenth century.

Mandarin: there are three names for this type of fan, which was made for the European market, which are either "Mandarin" or "Canton" or "Fan of a Thousand Faces". They are full of detail, exquisitely painted or appliquéd, and show the Western world what they hope to see of the East; busy scenes of various courts in China.

The leaves could be either of silk or of good quality hand-made paper, showing ladies and gentlemen of the court in multi-coloured clothes and holding fans. These clothes could be made of woven silk (probably from the Philippines) and applied to the leaf – sometimes you can run your little finger-nail around the edges of the garments, they are so beautifully done.

The faces (and, occasionally, the feet and hands) are made from minute slivers of ivory with the features painted upon them with a brush having only one hair…and those faces are so cleverly placed that they never balance across a pleat but rest in between.

The sticks are generally made of lacquered wood, round-shouldered and with no spaces in between, brilliantly gilded, or of heavily carved and fretted ivory, the guards always being carved in the round. The colouring, on the whole, is rich and deep, the leaf being in gentian blue, deep grass green or a brilliant fuchsia red, and the sticks of either black and gold lacquer, bright white ivory, multi-coloured lacquers (grey, brick-red, etc, in curious tooth-like shapes) or, just occasionally, of silver or gold filigree, touched with enamels.

These fans could have been made anywhere in China, incorporating silks from the Philippines and feathers or straw from the countryside; but they ended up by being exported from the port of Canton to Europe. Naturally no Chinese would dream of owning fans such as these as they would not be entitled to use a fan "outside their station".

Mai-ogi: Japanese dancing fans, with ten ribs, used between the seventeenth and twentieth centuries.

Maki-uchiwa: A roll-up or revolving fan, flat, used in the East.

Mita-ogi: A giant Japanese processional fan, about six to seven feet high.

Punkah: From "pankh", meaning "feather" or a bird, in an Indian dialect; this suggests the beating of a bird's wing to cool the air, and punkahs were generally made of either wood or fabric suspended from a heavy rod near the ceiling of a room and, with a series of ropes and pulleys, is pulled back and forth above a group of people by a servant. This allows the air to be slowly moved about. Dependent upon one's means the punkah would be either completely plain or elaborately decorated.

Sesata: a ceremonial standard fan from Sri Lanka.

Swatow: these fans came from the Chinese province of Kuangtung, and looked like a duck's foot. It was made from one single piece of bamboo, fastened across the middle with a strengthening piece of metal or leather. Then the upper section of bamboo was split into several sections, forced apart and held that way with rigid spacers between the sticks, and then fine paper was stretched over the sticks like the membrane of a duck's foot, and sometimes further decorated. These fans were named after Swatow, on the south coast, because so many were made there.

T'uan shan: see **Handscreen.**

Yamato-uchiwa: this is a fascinating form of rigid fan, made from two sheets of very fine silk or gauze or semi-transparent fine-grade paper, stretched over a rigid framework. Nothing decorates their outward parts at all. But, in the making of the fan, a decoration is slipped in between the two sheets; it could be a crab or a butterfly or a flower design. In daylight the fan looks quite plain, but, once held up to the candlelight or sunshine the ghost or spirit of the crab or butterfly seems enmeshed within, like a fly caught in a spider's web. The first of these appeared around the year 1800 in Yamato, which gives them their name.

There are a great many more fans' names in both China and Japan, but it would be wiser to read (if you can read modern Japanese with ease) Mr Kiyoe Nakamura's book on fans published recently in Japan. Mr Nakamura is famed as being the finest maker of fans in Japan today, and his family have plied that trade for several centuries.

Fans in the East were considered very thoughtfully and seriously, rigid protocol and custom marching hand in hand with artistic brilliance which is just becoming recognised by the western world today. Probably the finest time for the arts in Japanese history was during the period of the Tokugawa Shogunate (1603–1867) when the Japanese decided upon a policy of isolation.

I am indebted to Captain John A. Booth, U.S.A.F. retd., who spent a great many years in Japan, for the following informations about the making of history through a fan – which I have condensed:

"Around the year 1603, at the Shogun's castle in Yedo (now Tokyo) Tokugawa Ieyasu met all his ministers, counsellors, generals and courtiers to make a final decision about the presence of Dutch traders in Japan. The Tokugawa had just succeeded in unifying the war-torn nation (the Oda and Toyotomi period (1573–1603) was marked with nothing but civil strife), in liquidating the Christian missionaries and the Christian Japanese, and in imposing national isolation upon all the Japanese islands.

No-one, including Ieyasu, really wanted this last link with the outside world to be broken. How would they receive word that an invasion fleet was assembling to invade Nippon? The nation had never forgotten Kublai's attempt three centuries previously, nor the "Divine Wind" which had scattered his fleet, just as the English have never forgotten the Spanish attempt in 1588. Suppose the foreign barbarians should develop some new foods or animals or products which should be imported and developed in Japan for the improvement of their diet or clothing or shelter?

On the other hand thousands had died to enable the Shogun to sever all connections with the dangerous world outside, wherein savage men with pale faces, heavy beards, powerful guns and great ships were seizing all the islands and mainlands of the known world; if some foreigners were allowed to remain, despite severe penalties imposed on the Japanese for having anything to do with them, discontent and rebellion could arise again in the land. The people had just gone through a quarter of a century of civil war and wanted peace. Oda Nobunaga and Toyotomi Hideyoshi had raged all up and down the land – and disappeared – and now the people only wanted Ieyasu to give them peace within their own self-sufficient coasts. Should he, or should he not allow the Dutch to remain?

The Dutch could be trusted not to bring Jesuits or missionaries and subvert the people as the Portugese and Spanish had tried to do. The Dutch were pure and simple traders. Furthermore the port of Nagasaki on the Southern island of Kyushu seemed made for them: it was far from the Emperor (the impotent puppet in Kyoto) and farther from Yedo, the Shogun's capital, and it had a very long and narrow entrance. Any ship tying up at the innermost quay would be at the mercy of the Governor, and it could not depart without permission.

Tokugawa Ieyasu thought for a very long time.

Then he flung his fan down onto the floor and stalked out of the room without uttering a word.

Whichever of the two decisions he was implored to make would be wrong – so he made no decision. He was frustrated and angry and only he could give the word for which the court, the people and the Dutch traders were waiting so anxiously.

Since much of Japanese national policy had been, and would be, made by innuendo, by inference, by omens and by far-fetched interpretations the assemblage gathered round the fan to find a solution to the problem…were the Dutch, the last of the foreign merchants in Japan's ports, to be expelled or to be allowed to continue trading?

The courtiers carefully scrutinised the fan and found that it was lying open; this phenomenon they discussed and came to a consensus, without any one individual taking responsibility for a decision, to allow the Dutch to remain in Japan and to build them a trading zone in the shape of an outstretched fan.

This was done, and the Dutch remained there for the next two and a half centuries of Japanese isolation. A fill was made in the harbour, shaped like a fan without a handle, and all the necessary buildings of a trading post were built on it. It measured about three blocks by six, and Japanese guards were placed at one bridge. All Hollanders were kept inside and no Japanese were permitted on the island except those who were absolutely necessary, such as cooks, porters, housegirls etc; so, in effect, it was a prison for the Dutch.

Trading was very light over the years, the Dutch merely keeping the flag flying and hoping for better days. Only one ship was allowed in every four years and every four years the Dutch had to make a difficult overland pilgrimage along the road from Nagasaki to Yedo, subjected to scorn and ridicule by the Japanese, and then prostrate themselves before the ruling Tokugawa and ply him with gifts.

The Dutch trading post was called Dejima or Deshima ("shima" means island) and what had been waterfront in the seventeenth century was infilled in the nineteenth century and early twentieth century. However, tourist leaflets put out by Nagasaki today clearly show a painting of 1792 and the fan-shaped island used by the Dutch.

So, for two and a half centuries, history was determined by the toss of a fan".

Much has been written about Japanese fans, the important artists and the subjects for the compositions, complete with the paints or **sumi** techniques. Another type of fan, and a very collectable type at that, is the Nanga fan. Milne Henderson (99 Mount Street, London W.1.) generally has quite a few on exhibition, and they are available in America as well as in most other countries where there is any specialisation in Japanese art. .

John Hay wrote: "The art of Nanga, Southern School Painting, was once ignored or disdained by Western collectors or critics. There was a watershed in 1972, when the Asia House Gallery presented a major exhibition, and recently it has been arousing some of the interest it deserves. (Milne Henderson put on another Exhibition of Nanga Paintings in 1975, 1976 and 1978). This interest will undoubtedly endure, for the Nanga school is one of the most accessible areas of Japanese painting. It is near at hand, having grown to maturity in the late eighteenth century; then, for over a century, through it were channelled much of the period's artistic energies. Unlike Ukiyo-e, its principal rival for attention, its essential quality is personal and so it increasingly rewards intimate acquaintance.

"In the history of art it is of great interest because it sought, in part, to create a Japanese extension of the Chinese "Southern School". This was traditionally amateur painting of the scholar-gentleman, which in China had already a history of many centuries. Interest in it arose out of the last great surge of Chinese cultural influence in Japan. For some, this same historical context has made Nanga painting seem academic and distant. But the reverse is the case. Whilst the *literati* tradition in China had already become dangerously extended, in Japan it provided a fresh challenge and provoked much that was original. The Chinese dimension may be ignored without lessening the achievements of Nanga, or it may be considered as an added interest.

"In Tokugawa Japan, the intensive study of Chinese culture created a desire to live its art as an integral function to understanding it. It brought also an increasing knowledge of actual works by Chinese scholar artists. During the eighteenth century, much of such knowledge was drawn from Chinese woodcut painting manuals and the influence of these is clearly visible in design, motif and brush formula. During the later decades of the

eighteenth century, more original paintings were seen and, further, a few Chinese artists actually taught in Japan. Simultaneously, artists of genius working in the new Nanga tradition began creating styles of tremendous originality such as Chikudō, Gyokudō, Hyakusen and Taiga. Their followers have been somewhat overshadowed, but fans by Gyokuran, Gyokushū and Kaikai show that they were major artists who deserve much closer attention.

"Around the turn of the century, as the nature of Chinese sources became clearer, increasingly orthodox traditions were established. It is possible to line up successive formulizations of a particular manner, such as that of the fourteenth century Chinese artist Ni Tsan – a process that may unexpectedly highlight the individuality of the painters involved. The changes over these decades often come between the work of fathers and sons, such as Okada Beisanjin and Hankō, Uragami Gyokudō and Shunkin. As in the case of Shunkin, paintings of flowers and birds and related subjects show

well the way in which decorative tendencies merged with Chinese manners.

"In Kyoto and Osaka, orthodox trends were particularly strong and were related to the development of orthodox Confucian studies. These often centred round the great scholar Rai San'yō. He was a fine calligrapher and a somewhat staid painter. Among his colleagues and students were many Nanga artists.

Nanga penetrated the more eclectic and pragmatic circles of Edo rather more slowly; when it did so the results were no less impressive. The orthodox tendencies of the nineteenth century did not, however, mean any lack of stature or variety among the artists as a whole. Just as Nanga artists and their Chinese forbears used the writing brush as the perfect instrument with which to express their personality, so Nanga painting is a most rewarding world for one's personal exploration."

Chikuden is one of the most highly regarded of all the Nanga painters, the ultimate Japanese *bunjin*, living from

1777–1835. His health was always poor and he had to give up his ambition to become a Confucian scholar. However he travelled far and made many friends such as Bunchō, Rai San'yō and many others, remaining amongst the most scholarly of the Nanga artists, being at his best in small compositions.

Since his death the reputation of Gyokudō has risen more than that of any other Nanga master. This has been especially true in recent decades and his work has roused much excitement in the West. He lived from 1745–1820 and in 1794 he flouted convention by going away on a sight-seeing tour with his sons and resigning his responsibilities as a retainer in the Ikeda clan. He then appears to have taught himself to paint, maturing slowly and becoming a master of the realization of the abstract. He was the father of Shunkin.

Top. *18th century fan, probably English, painted with figures in a garden. The ivory sticks are pierced, carved and painted. c. 1760. Chinoiserie guards.*
Left. *Japanese Nanga fan. "Landscape – with two lines of poetry" by Matsudaira Shungaku (1828-90). Ink and light colours on paper. Inscription: "Leaning on his oar is a poet – not returning; the misty waters of the lake become his home". 'Shunggaku'. Seal: 'Tsugusugi'.*
Top right. *Japanese Nanga fan – "Travelling through Cold Mountains", painted by Satake Kaikai (1738-90), ink on paper.*
Centre right. *Japanese Nanga fan – "River landscape with pine and sailing boats" by Ikeno Gyokuran (1728-84) – ink on 'glittering' paper.*
Bottom right. *Japanese folding fan. "Ise-ebi" (Lobster) by Zeshin (1807-91). This fan shows a most imaginative use of the space available.*
Overleaf. *The reverse of the fan shown at the top of the page, depicting a Chinoiserie scene.*

Hyakusen is thought to have been of Chinese descent; although he is usually counted as one of the three pioneering masters of Nanga, together with Gion Nankai and Yanagisawa Kien, he differed from these other two by professedly being a complete professional. The range of his styles was extraordinarily wide and the exact extent to which he and other painters like him studied original Chinese paintings is impossible to determine – much of their material came from either Chinese woodblock prints or inferior copies. However, in his work, Hyakusen always uses a dramatic approach to composition which is typically Japanese.

Ikeno Taiga and his contemporary are admired as the two greatest masters of Nanga; the breadth and stature of his character is more fully matched in the greatness of his art than is the case with any other artist of the school. He was born in 1723 (d.1776) in a small village just north of Kyoto, showing much talent as an artist – and, during the early part of his life, opened a fan shop and sold large numbers of fans in the Gion park to establish his name. There he met his wife, Gyokuran, daughter of a tea-seller and had such friends as Kaikai, the sake-seller and fan-painter.

Kuwayama Gyokushū (1746–1799) has an interesting position in the development of Nanga styles, for he was a writer on theoretical issues who also expressed himself in painting with considerable originality. He was the first to associate the Rimpa painters with "Southern School" ideals and his painting shows a conscious concern with their decorative values. He was a close friend and pupil of Taiga and found his artistic home in Kyoto.

Satake Kaikai although fifteen years younger than Taiga, (he lived 1738–1790), is said to have met him while the latter was selling fans in the Gion Park and Kaikai was himself running a sake stall. He became an artist of strength and originality and his work is nowadays rare but highly regarded.

There are many other artists in the Nanga School, most of whose lives have been recorded and documented (especially in James Cahill's book *Scholar Painters of Japan: The Nanga School*, the Asia Society Inc, 1972) but the point which must emphatically be made is that these artists are all known and most have signed their work, in direct contrast to the painters of fans in the Western world, where a signature is both a surprise and very suspect during the eighteenth century. It is extremely important to make this point about *craft* in the West and *art* in the East.

Prices of Oriental fans vary very much indeed, for there are simply very few of them available for sale in the Western world. Famous galleries are pleased if they have more than half a dozen a year of exceptional quality and by top-ranking artists to show to prospective customers. Nevertheless it is possible to buy a good fan for $160. Prices show a slow but steady movement upward each year.

To buy a pretty good Chinese fan painting (although obviously not by the most famous of the old Court painters) one would start by paying about $500. For fans

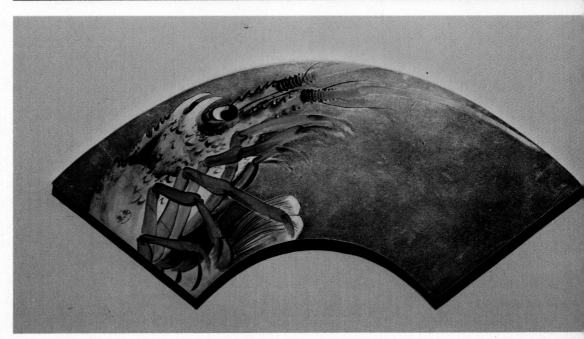

painted by some members of the Nanga School there is a much greater variation, the average being about $700 and the scale, as a whole, stretching from $300 to $3,000.

The most expensive fan painting Milne Henderson has ever sold was one by Uragami Gyokudō (1745–1820) for a total of $9,000, and is pictured on the cover of the catalogue of "Nanga Fan Painting". As Mrs Henderson pointed out, this is not all that much money to pay out for a painting in

these days. Fan collectors, however, have never been known to pay that amount for Western European fans, but cheerfully pay out much more for a Constable or a Turner. I feel it gives one a great deal of food for thought.

Other fans from the East are well-covered in the book published by Debretts Peerage for the 1978/9 Exhibition "Fans from the East". There are five sections: "Fans from Japan", "Fans from China", "Chinoiserie",

"Fans from the Seychelles to the Philippines" and "A Living Art". There are many illustrations and explanations of types, both in the arts and in the crafts; the authors are the people who mounted each section of the Exhibition – Joe Earle, Julia Hutt, Nancy Armstrong and Katy Talati.

Lace Fans

Many a nineteenth century fan is made up of lace, sometimes with the addition of silk, gauze or taffeta, and, for catalogue purposes, or if they wish to sell their fans privately, owners may wish to know what types of lace have been used.

As Patricia Wardle puts it in her excellent book *Victorian Lace* (pub: Herbert Jenkins, London, 1968) "Lace of the nineteenth century has been somewhat neglected by modern writers. In fact, most people, rather hastily, dismiss it as being inferior in both design and quality to laces of earlier centuries and, thus, lacking in interest in comparison with them. Yet probably there was no century in which lace was so much admired and used as in the nineteenth, and certainly more lace survives from this period than from any other".

The Victorian lady found lace had to be worn (if not upon her dresses at least upon her underwear) throughout most of the century. Machines eventually made lace very beautifully, and everyone who was able collected antique lace as well. Lace remained extremely expensive, as it always had been, but, in the past, it had generally been reserved for the wealthy members of Court

Top left. *Japanese Nanga fan. "Landscape, trees and mountains with temple in mist – with poem" by Nukina Kaioku (1778-1863). Ink on paper. Inscription and seals.*
Top centre left. *Chinese folding fan – ink and light colour on paper. "Crossing by ferry on an autumn evening" and "In the year* hsin-ssu *(1881?) 9th moon; at the elegant request of respected elder P'ei-chich; may he correct it; Kan-hsia, Yeh Wen-chung". Seal: Ku-chuan, 19th century.*
Bottom centre left. *Chinese folding fan; ink and light colours on gold-covered paper. "Asking for elucidation of a new poem" – "Something in the manner of a Yüan dynasty artist; staying at Shen-chiang; Shao-hsiang". Seal: "Wen-ch'un". The artist of this very elegant fan has not been identified.*
Bottom left. *Japanese Nanga fan. "Bodhidharma" – painted by Ikeno Taiga (1723-76); ink on paper. Signed "Kasho" with two seals of the artist.*
Top right. *Chinese folding fan; ink on gold-dusted paper, no signature or seal. This fan, probably of the 18th century, is a typical example of the free ink play cultivated by the scholar-calligrapher. It is reminiscent of the 17th century artists such as Cha Shih-piao.*
Bottom right. *Chinese folding fan; ink and touches of colour on paper. "Scholar's studio deep among willows. In the year* chi-ssu *(1809) summer; at the elegant request of my old brother P'ei-ch'u; Ch'ing-pai Tao-jen, Chou Chi did this in the San-yüan hall at Yang-shih". Seal: Chou Chi.*

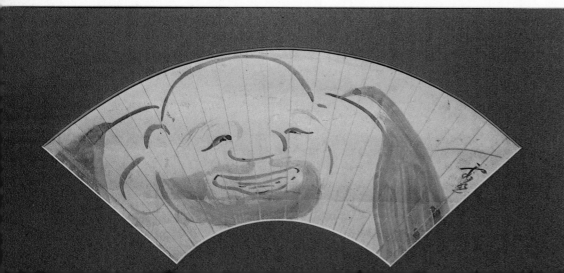

or Society – now it could be bought and worn by anyone who had the wherewithal. In 1862 (at the International Exhibition in London) Brussels lace squares sold for twenty dollars, black real point lace flouncings were from thirty-six dollars and "imitation" point lace flouncings were from four dollars. In 1874 the price for Honiton lace bridal veils was from ten to a hundred dollars *upwards*, and fans from four to twenty-four dollars.

Lace was a great source of income through its supply and demand: P. L. Simmonds wrote in the *Art Journal* of 1872 that Britain exported nearly two million dollars' worth of cotton lace and almost as much of silk lace. To balance that there were

imports of lace to the tune of $1,500,000, almost equally divided between machine-lace and pillow-lace; and it is just this see-sawing between hand-made and machine-made lace which is a fascinating feature of that century.

Ladies liked machine-made goods because they were a novelty, yet they insisted on standards of quality which, until the third quarter of the century, the machine could not attain.

Eighteenth century lace fans are exceptionally rare and one should not accept out of hand that small lace fans minus loops or ribbons are from that era – their loops may have been removed long ago – for most lace fans are of the nineteenth century. Equally it

is a mistake to feel that all lace fans are bridal fans, they need not be, and one should remember that bridal white was far from regulation wear during the Victorian era. Small lace fans could easily have been made for young girls coming out or for all-purpose dance fans which would adapt to many dresses in the days when lace frills and furbelows were fashionable.

There are very few definite rules about fans and it is possible that there are too many sweeping statements about dating fans through costume. Contemporary illustrations show the general size of a fan (small in the 1810's, large in the 1880's) which was expected to be used by the lady of fashion. But

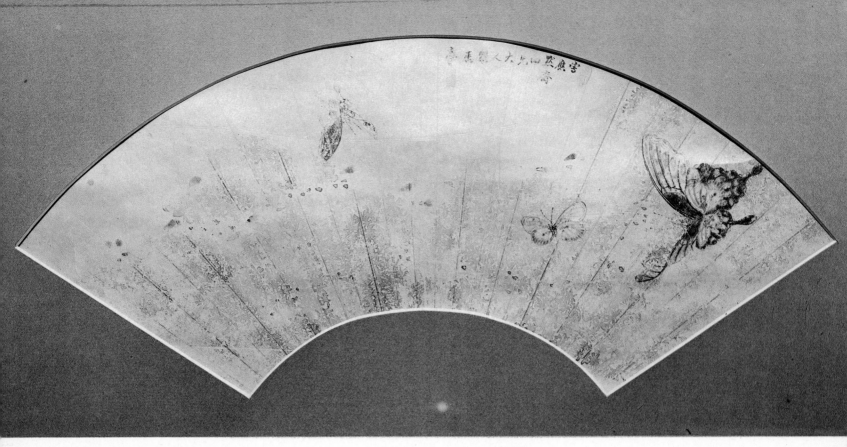

everyone was not rich, and many a member of the landed gentry or aristocracy may have felt it looked ostentatious to use the latest styles and, instead, commissioned fans which hankered back to the past. This also accounts for the amount of replacing of new leaves (loose copies of treasured Georgian designs) onto old sticks or vice versa. There has never been an era when some section of society has not had to economise and this reason, together with the antipathy towards the new (and vulgar?) rich women, benefiting from their brash husbands' expertise during the Industrial Revolution, has resulted in some muddled dating of nineteenth century fans.

Economy also accounts for the good condition of questionable fans, for poor but genteel ladies looked after their precious "made over" fans with greatest care, where their richer sisters could toss away a carelessly treated fashionable one.

Lace has always been expensive, has always been "for show" and, therefore, has always been placed upon sticks of ivory or mother-of-pearl (when white) and generally tortoiseshell when black or *ecru*, but never of wood. A special point to look for is whether the lace has been adapted for a fan or been especially made for one. Sometimes beautiful old lace, which can be used again and again for different purposes, was placed upon a fan and, in order to adapt to the sticks, a small pleat or tuck was made at the top by the guards.

A lace leaf is quite another thing: where the lace is made in a curved shape, the design has a carefully balanced border and the sticks are made to adapt to the lace. There is a world of difference between the two.

In order to obtain advice about types of lace it is generally possible to enquire at your local Museum, especially if it has a costume section. If you live in the London area it is best to go to the Textile Department of the Victoria and Albert Museum on a Tuesday or a Thursday afternoon when free advice is given... *but never valuations.* Telephone in advance to make an appointment.

Fashions in lace during the nineteenth century.

For the first twenty years lace was light, to go with the classically inspired clothes, without any heavy patterns but often with a net-like appearance and little spots or flowers dotted over the ground. One found classical scrolls or Greek key-fret motifs, and sometimes vases or urns in the lace designs; the straight edges eventually giving way (c.1815) to scallops or Vandyke points.

The next fifty years began to see inventiveness and colour, especially in black silk laces and *blonde.* The designs soon became ornate and heavy, and one should especially remember that a Victorian lady was happy to have contrasts on her costume. A gaily-coloured dress (or even a deeply coloured one) would have white lace to touch up and give it life, and so she would carry a white lace fan. Very rarely was a lace fan made to match an outfit... matching accessories is more of a twentieth century idea. Equally, a dress of matt-textured fabric would require a sleekly silky fan and a satin dress would look best with a patterned lace fan, for contrast of texture was as important as contrast of colour. Herein lie some of the pitfalls of fan-dating.

Black and white silk lace fans were fashionable in the 1850's and 1860's, some being very heavy and rather coarse but cheaper than their lighter counterparts because they were easier to make. This was the hey-day of Maltese lace, Chantilly, Brussels and (for the very rich) Alençon needlepoint – one associates them all with the stylish Empress Eugénie. By the end of the 1860's one finds the more gauzy, filmy laces, and from the 1870's to 1900 the machine-made laces came into their own, especially for fans. The colours were black or white and, in 1870, the beginning of the vogue for *écru*, which went on into the twentieth century. By the 1870's Honiton or Brussels lace became almost a uniform for brides, with matching fans at last, the prices of each type being roughly the same. You could pay between one to ten guineas for a pocket handkerchief trimmed with Honiton lace in those days.

In the 1880's showy lace came back into fashion, but with patterns often copied from the seventeenth century, and fans were so large that the lightest types such as Chantilly, Mechlin and Brussels *point de gaze* had to be used in case the huge leaf broke the mother-of-pearl sticks – the laces being mainly machine-made. Sometimes the lace was also dyed to match the sweet-pea colours of the lovely dresses.

Right at the end of the century there was a little Art Nouveau lace, but not very much was used for fans: ladies preferred ostrich feathers instead. It seems worthwhile to examine, briefly, the basic techniques of lace-making but it must be remembered throughout that there is a slight problem in the naming of the types. In the sixteenth to eighteenth centuries laces were named after the towns in which they were made (i.e. Chantilly, Alençon, Brussels etc) but by the nineteenth century these were merely *types* of laces, and could be made in many other places: Brussels lace, in other words, might be made in any area of Belgium; Chantilly could also be made in Caen, Bayeux or Belgium; Alençon lace in Brussels or even Burano, and Honiton lace in Ireland.

Needlepoint lace

The main nineteenth century needlepoint laces in constant use were Venetian, Alençon, Argentan and Brussels *point de gaze*; they all share the basic techniques but, to the professional eye looking through a magnifying glass, they can be told apart through their looped background stitches. The method was as follows:-

Take two thicknesses of material and sew

your carefully designed pattern onto them. This pattern need not be the finished article, for there is no limit to the size of needlepoint laces, yet in the case of a fan the pattern was probably for the whole leaf. There are very few good fan leaves of lace with merely a repetitive design upon them, they show instead a complete design of a central theme surrounded by an elaborately scrolled or flowered border. No longer (as with some painted fans) are they treated as rectangular paintings with the corners cut off for the curves and a central section removed for the sticks; a lace fan leaf was treated far more like the Orientals treated their fan leaves, working in one curving flow of movement and considered all of a piece.

Your two pieces of fabric, complete with the surface design, are then attached to a framework in order to keep the tension even. After this all one needs are lengths of thread, a needle or two and some fine scissors. Take your needle and thread and cover the outlines of your design with lines of thread which are held in place (anywhere where the direction changes) by another thread passed over them and right through the pattern and the two layers of fabric underneath. This outlining, making a skeleton upon which to work (infilling, cutting out, thickening outlines etc) is called *"le trace"*. Once the skeleton is formed then the real work is done where the lace-maker infills the designs, some worked almost into a solid area, others in a freer, more open stitchery, without exception by the use of tiny buttonhole stitches.

A raised edge to a motif *("la brode")* and a variety of fancy infilling stitches *("les modes")* gradually builds up the entire picture; where you have a dominant motif which has to be joined to another area you have buttonholed

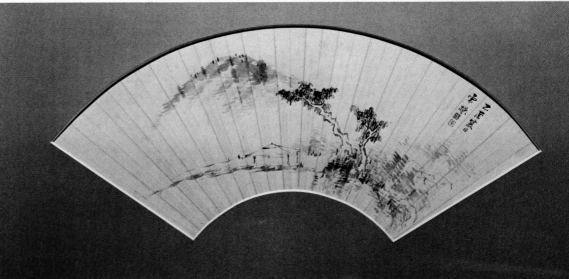

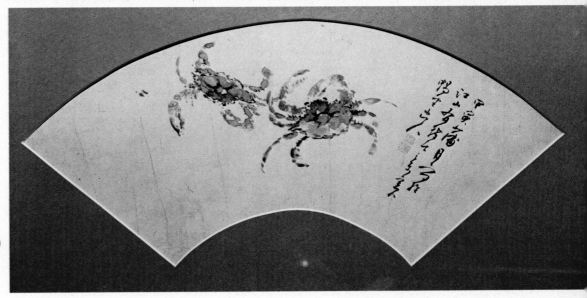

Top left. *Chinese folding fan; ink and colours on paper. "Written at the elegant request of Mei-chai"– signature illegible. The painting of butterflies and flower petals in a breeze is often associated with fans, for the association is an obvious one. Two popular Chinese terms for a fan are: 'to call the wind' and 'to strike a butterfly'. Probably a 19th century fan.*

Top right. *Chinese folding fan; gold on blue paper. "Wang Hui-chih, who planted bamboos all around his house, said that he could not be without this gentleman for a single day. The year ting-ssu (1797) at the beginning of summer, wiping away the sweat; inspired by the manner of Hsüeh-weng (Old Snowman); at the most elegant request of respected elder (?)-ch'un; Sung-yen, Chou Kan".*

Top centre right. *Japanese Nanga fan. "Landscape, Pavilion under trees" painted by Kaneko Sesso (1794-1857). Ink and colour on paper. Inscription: "1852, a summer day; Sesso". Seals: 'Kaku', 'Han'.*

Bottom centre right. *Japanese Nanga fan. "Two crabs" by Maeda Chodo (1878-78), ink and colour on paper. Inscription: "1854…chodo-sanjin". Seals: "Hirokazu-in," "Jitsuho."*

Bottom right. *Chinese folding fan – ink on gold covered paper. "Jen-tzu (1852?), a spring day; written for Hsing-ch'a's correction: Jen-mao (?), Feng Chien". Seal: "Nung-yu". The little scholar hidden away in a mountain hut makes an effective fan, which demonstrates the difficulty of imbuing with life the tones of ink on a shiny, coloured paper.*

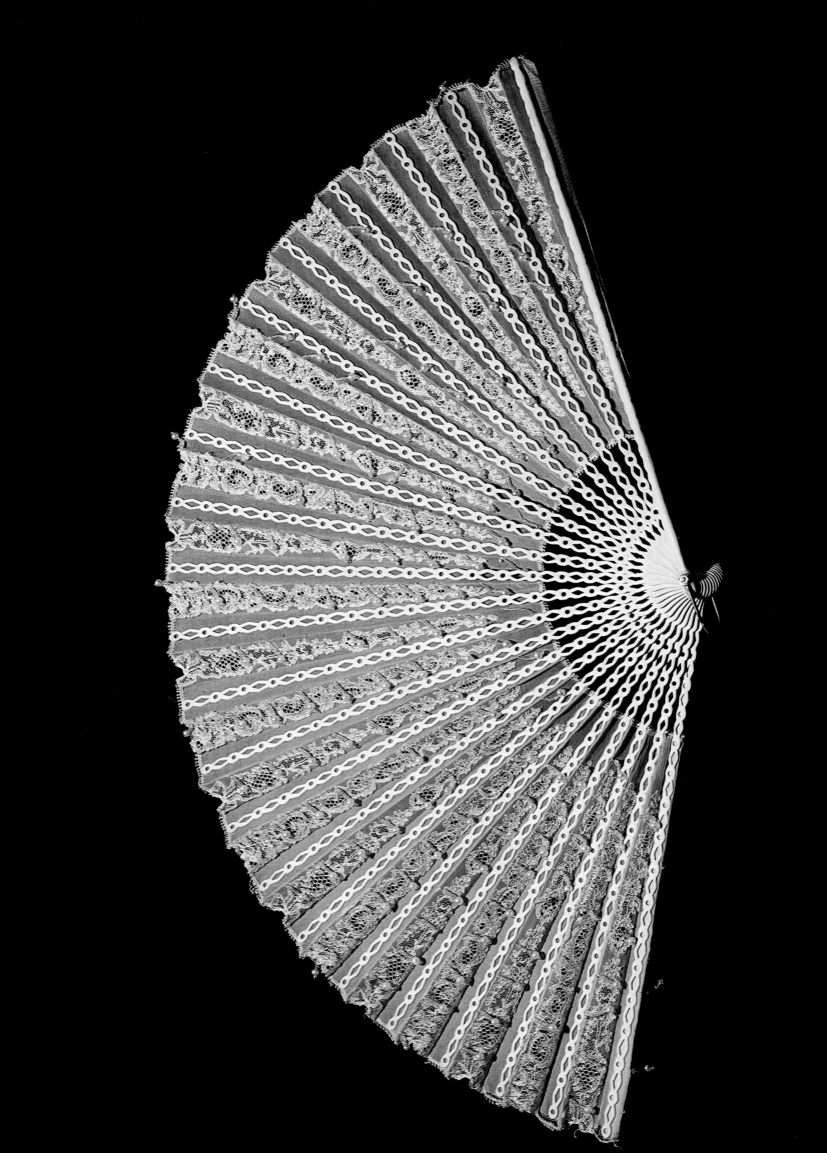

bars ("brides") and you can also have enrichment through small needle-made dots ("picots") or even by various forms of mesh grounds. Sometimes several recognisable techniques are used at the same time, which is known as "mixed lace" – but this is no disparagement. When the entire design is finished the lace fan-leaf is detached from the underlying pattern and layers of fabric by snipping the little anchoring threads between the two layers of fabric which frees the whole film of lace. So much work has been done over the threads that they hold themselves together, yet it is obvious that the designer should also know some of the techniques in order that the tension of threads is reasonably even in the finished article.

To recognise the types mentioned above one notices (under a glass) that Venetian needlepoint laces have a background of brides; Brussels point de gaze (a beautiful gauzy lace as the name suggests) has a very fine background network of simply looped threads; Alençon has a ground of square meshes with twisted sides, and Argentan has a hexagonal mesh of which the sides are entirely covered by buttonhole stitching.

Bobbin lace. (Or Pillow-lace, the names are interchangeable.)

The method with bobbin lace is to have a round or square pillow, endless threads, a great many bobbins (partly used as weights), a pattern marked out on a piece of fine, strong vellum or card, exceptional eyesight and unending patience.

The pattern generally shows one repeat of the design to be worked, which makes fan-making extremely difficult because a fan-leaf really needs to be worked as a whole. Thus bobbin-lace leaves for fans probably have several designs on several separate pieces of vellum or card; partly for the scalloped edges, partly for the upper areas and finally even smaller motifs for the area near the sticks.

The pattern needs to be pricked through the parchment by an expert, for these holes will take the pins around which the threads will gradually become plaited or looped together, independent of any supporting material. As the pattern is small it is going to be used again and again, so the greatest accuracy in the first pricking-through is essential.

Secure the pattern on to the pillow. Then put in the first series of pins firmly and attach the threads to them, the remainder of the length of thread being wound around a weight (the bobbin) which hangs down over the edge of the pillow like the branches of a weeping willow tree.

Then you either cross the threads over one another or twist them together to form the miniscule pattern in front of you on the parchment, every now and again putting in a pin to change direction or anchor a

Left. *Fine English fan, the gauze leaf having lace inserts and tiers of strung pearls and beads sewn onto the folds of the fan. Sticks of white painted wood, elaborately pierced. c. 1890.*
Overleaf. *An Art Nouveau fan showing a peacock painted onto both the paper leaf and the wooden sticks. English. c. 1905.*

movement. So you make your design which can be one long continuous series of flowers or scrolls, for instance, or can be merely a simple net-like area. If you make a whole collection of similar designs, say a bouquet of flowers, for instance, and finish them off and *then* join them all together to form a fan-leaf by simple connecting bars (brides) without any net-like effect at all, this is called "guipure" lace.

You can also have a net background worked into the spaces between the motifs, even some elaborately fancy fillings; these include Brussels bobbin lace, which has a net ground of hexagonal meshes, with two sides plaited and four twisted, showing a characteristic openwork edge which appears around all the motifs. Or you can have *Honiton* bobbin lace, which is very much like Brussels, but without the hexagonal mesh.

Torchon is the simplest lace: beginners stumble their way through this elementary process, where a coarse net ground is made and geometric patterns are worked on this. *Plaited laces* are simple interwoven lines of plaited threads and, although normally thought of as part of the earliest geometrically patterned laces of the sixteenth and seventeenth centuries, they enjoyed a revival in the late nineteenth century. Sometimes lace had to begin and end with the same amount of threads, working continuously and evenly, with no threads either added or subtracted from beginning to end. These are known as "continuous thread" laces and usually have to have a straight edge.

Valenciennes. This has a strong net ground of diamond-shaped mesh, all four sides of which are plaited, with a very solidly woven pattern area (toilé). Valenciennes was a part of the ancient province of Hainault in the Netherlands, becoming French in the late seventeenth century. They had their best years from 1725 to 1780, when there were four thousand lacemakers in the area. After the French Revolution, in 1790, there were only two hundred and fifty lacemakers left and by 1851 there were but two.

The designs of Valenciennes (and "Binche") were so complicated and closely worked that they took an enormous amount of time. *Binche* is made on the same lines but is more gauzy in appearance, with looser-woven motifs arranged, sometimes, into a ground of round spots.

Mechlin. The background is a net of six-sided meshes, two sides being plaited and the other four twisted. Then the motifs worked in have an outline of thick thread, giving a certain sculptured effect. *Mechlin* was very expensive and therefore very popular at the court of Louis XV. All early Flemish laces were known as *Mechlin*, and were mainly made at Antwerp, Lierre and Turnhout; it was rich to look at, could have a scalloped edge and looked very pretty if placed over a coloured fabric.

Lille is similar to *Mechlin*, with its thick outlining of the motif, but with a light net ground with hexagonal meshes where the sides are all twisted and none are plaited. This lace originated in France during the eighteenth century and was in great demand during the nineteenth, when it was made in both cotton and linen thread.

Point de Paris is a net ground for laces in

which the meshes seem to form little six-pointed stars, because basically the meshes of the net are twisted and not plaited. It started life in Paris in the eighteenth century and then moved to Belgium; the very delicate designs invariably show flowers, baskets, birds and cherubs – just the sort of thing which would appeal to Victorian ladies. *East Midlands* laces and *blonde* (made of cream-coloured silk) were all worked like *Lille* or *Point de Paris.*

Chantilly was a favourite lace for fine fans, made from black silk and worked the same as *blonde.* A manufactory was begun at Chantilly in the seventeenth century by Catherine de Roban, duchesse de Longueville; then it died at the time of the French Revolution (it was, after all, under royal patronage) but started up again at both Caen and Bayeux by 1835. The finest lace leaves were often made of *Chantilly* black silk bobbin lace, a very difficult process it was, too, to create a curved area with a continuous thread lace normally making a straight or scalloped edge.

In needlepoint lace possibly the finest was made of *Brussels point de gaze.* Between that and *Youghal* needlepoint lace is a quite extraordinary difference, both using much the same techniques but *Brussels* being better and *Youghal* more prolific.

The lace industry in Ireland did not really become widespread until the famine years of the late 1840's. How strange to think that making lace was introduced into Ireland as a measure of famine-relief, when everyone knew that the lace-making industry was in a decline! But it paid off! By the 1851 Exhibition Irish lace was nothing to be ashamed of at all. Most of it was made by starving free-lance women with a dozen mouths to feed, almost no direction and with utmost difficulties as to sales outlets. But they perservered and many people bought rather dull Irish lace as a patriotic gesture to help the poor.

The most influential centre formed to teach Irish needlepoint lace (both cotton and linen) was at the Presentation Convent in Youghal, County Cork; it was opened in 1852 and was still going strong by the end of the century, all the lace being sold through the Irish Lace Depot in Dublin. Bobbin lace in Ireland was neither as prolific nor as popular, although some was made on the lines of *Honiton. Limerick* lace is neither bobbin nor needlepoint, it is an embroidered machine-made net, the embroidery being either "tamboured" (chain-stitch embroidery) or *needlerun.*

The History of Machine-wrought Lace and Hosiery Manufactures, by William Felkin, published in 1867 gives the rise and fall of factory production in the greatest detail; *Nottingham Lace,* by Zillah Halls, published by the Castle Museum in Nottingham, 1964, is far more palatable. In the second half of the eighteenth century inventors attempted to make a lace-like fabric on a machine, the first patent for making a type of net on a stocking machine was taken out in 1764. Endless variations on this theme took place where attempts were made to create a hexagonal net mesh with twisted sides, and success seemed assured when John Heathcoat took out his patent in 1808.

Improvements and modifications went on and on until, in 1830, a good, regular *Lille*-like mesh-net was produced – and produced in any width you wanted. The bobbin-net machine was also invented, so patterned machine-made lace could develop. Machine-made laces of both types see-sawed wildly as over-production produced a glut or a new machine was invented and the others went out of fashion until, at the end of the 1830's there came the greatest breakthrough of them all…a Jacquard apparatus was attached to the machines so that patterns could be produced purely mechanically. Now the workers could run off all sorts of imitation laces – *Valenciennes, Mechlin, blonde, Brussels* and so on.

The result? Down tumbled the price. At the Great Exhibition of 1851 it was noted by the Jury Panel for laces "that a yard of four-quarter white silk *blonde*, which in 1830 sold for 2s., is now suppled for 6d."

After 1860 the imitations became so good that it was difficult to tell the difference, and by the end of the century a great many hand-made laces were at an end, for the machines had conquered the markets.

Western European Varnished or Japanned Fans

It is essential that the subject of *vernis Martin* fans should be reviewed in a new light, bearing in mind the careful researches of Dr Hans Huth in his recent book *Lacquer in the West: The History of a Craft and an Industry, 1550-1950.* (The University of Chicago Press, 1971.)

So many fans are called *vernis Martin* and yet there is not a shred of evidence that the Martin family ever signed a single item of their varnished wares from furniture to fans; many fans with "their" technique are of poor quality and it would be a crime in many instances to associate them with this prestigious family.

In the recent past it has become generally agreed that this term would cover all early eighteenth century fans which were, in the main, of a brisé type with varnished or japanned sticks over a painted decoration. I feel that, in all fairness, the term should be altered to either "brisé japanned" or "brisé varnished" for European fans, and "brisé lacquered" for Oriental fans – and that the poor Martin family should be left alone to reap the rewards of the marvellous items they are known to have made in France… which just *might* have included fan sticks.

There now remains the difficult question as to whether France was the home of the varnishing industry and if not, where else can we look? I have no wish to denigrate the magnificent teams of workers in France, but so many fans (as opposed to the incomparable furniture) have what are laughingly called *vernis Martin* techniques, yet are of a quality which any Frenchman would blanch to call "Made in Paris". Yet they must have come from somewhere, so we should consider other sources for their making.

So what is the background of lacquer and varnish? And why was there a gap in the use of japanned objects from about 1630 to 1650? And should we consider these early dates at all? Personally I feel some japanned fans should have an earlier date than they are given today, partly because people associate them with the Martin family and, knowing their dates, feel they could not have been made earlier. There is a vast field here for research where identification could as easily be made through the painted leaf as the varnished sticks.

According to Dr Huth, and most major furniture historians, there were two waves of influence from the East upon the West. The first, a short one lasting only from about 1550 to 1630, came from the Near East and made Venice the earliest manufacturing centre in Europe of japanned objects. The second wave, by far the more important, beginning about 1650, was marked by the impact of the Far East and has lasted until modern times. This launched Europe into the great era of *chinoiseries* and consequent widespread attempts to imitate lacquer.

These two waves certainly seem to solve the puzzle of the gap in the mid-seventeenth century between the first appearance of japanned wares in Europe which put down no roots and faded away, and the sudden burst of activity in trade and manufacture in the last third of the century. In England this lack of continuity has been attributed to the Civil War and Interregnum, but we now know that it was a European phenomenon.

Strangely interesting is the role that England had to play in all this, for Dr Huth points out that lacquer was a more important element in furniture and decoration in England than in any other European country. England thus naturally took the lead in the manufacture of japanned wares and her trading connections took these goods to many parts of Europe and to North America. European countries with a seaboard were inevitably open to contact with Oriental products and substitute articles, and many of these countries had close trading links with England. They stretched from Spain and Portugal to Norway. Holland, Germany and Italy (especially Venice, Naples and Genoa) also had a strong and sustained demand for English japanning, examples of which were used as models for their own manufactures. France, of course, remained – as ever – the exception. She began to develop her own japanned wares, impervious to developments in England, shortly after 1650, reaching the climax with the famous *vernis Martin* which was used to decorate some of the greatest achievements of the royal ébénistes. Yet even this high quality work could not match the brilliance or durability of genuine lacquer.

It is, therefore, extremely important for fan collectors to be able to differentiate between lacquering, japanning and varnishing. It is also of interest to point out the various centres – and schools – in each country, and to give dates where possible.

What, then, is the difference between genuine lacquer and European japanning and varnishing? The short answer is "ingredients and ignorance." Both are mediums in which a resin has been made soluble by the addition of suitable ingredients before application, in several coatings, to objects decorated in colour.

Lacquer

In the Orient there was an almost religious feeling about the quality of lacquer and the meticulous application of it. The tree from which the resin was collected is now known as *rhus vernicifera*, a variety of the sumac family, called *Ch'ichou* in China and *Urishi-no-ki* in Japan. Europeans in the eighteenth century called it either *Tsi, Ci* or *Chiram* in their tracts.

The resin was, incidentally, particularly irritating to the skin and had to be applied in dustless conditions. According to Dr Huth the lacquer-worker would wear as few clothes as possible so that the dust from them could not settle on the tacky lacquer as it dried; he would also seal the door to his workshop or even, in extreme cases, take to a boat and row far out to sea for the same reason.

In the *Diary of an Art Dealer* by René Gimpel (New York 1966) there was an account by Jean Dunand working in the Oriental technique early in this century "…So you have to varnish or lacquer twenty times – or rather forty, as the job has to be repeated on the other side to keep the wood from warping; otherwise it would crack, for you wouldn't believe how easily the lacquer can twist even the hardest wood into a semi-circle. Actually not forty but as many as a hundred preparations are required since after each varnishing you have to polish and before each varnishing there have to be twenty seasonings, each lasting four days… (they)…require damp conditioning, and a dark room where water flows continuously".

As the European workers had never seen the Orientals at work in the seventeenth and eighteenth centuries it must excuse them from knowing the exact amount of care, trouble and time that they should have employed. Nor did they know that lacquer was both used as a protective and decorative varnish or, when solidified, as a medium for sculpture. Because of this lack of intimate knowledge it becomes obvious that European varnishing techniques never rivalled those of the Orient.

The European word "lacquer" comes from shellac, a resin and a true lacquer ingredient, which was also called *gomma lacca* or *lacca*. Since shellac contains a red pigment which could only be eliminated by a process discovered after 1770, *lacca* frequently stands for "red colour". (Another pitfall to collectors).

Actually the original word shellac takes its name from the Sanskrit *Lakh*, meaning one hundred thousand – used monetarily in India today, as in 'a lakh of rupees' – in other words it means "almost innumerable". And wh…

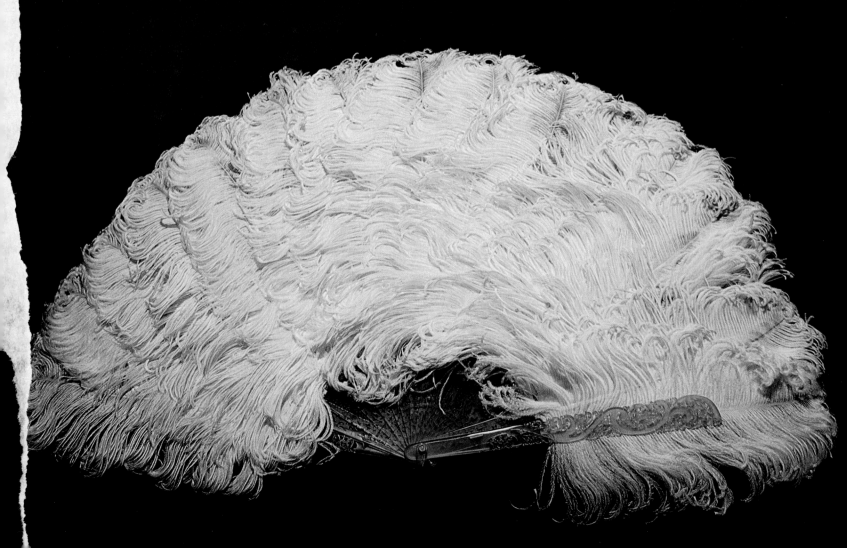

silk leaf, painted with three vignettes showing delightful amorini playing on the moon (possibly a "honeymoon" fan) surrounded by very fine creamy lace as frames and with mother-of-pearl sticks and guards.

Two of the sticks were broken and one of the guards; and every single fold of the silk, back and front, was split from top to bottom. Only the creamy lace "frames" appeared undamaged which was not surprising as the whole mess was sent to us wrapped in a single plastic bag in an envelope. We were naturally reluctant to touch the fan, especially as we had no idea how much had been damaged in the post – advice on packing fans is included later on in this chapter.

Finally, after long consultation with several craftsmen, we put forward a solution to the owner. We suggested that the three scenes should be taken off, mended and then put into Hogarth frames as though they were individual paintings, the sticks repaired and the lace renewed. This is how we did it:

1. We removed, with a new razor blade, every stitch which held the lace onto the silk; this was a very good lesson about Victorian patience, as it took three days altogether.

2. We then made templates for the lace "frames", washed each of them – as explained above, and left them to dry on clean white blotting paper.

3. Then we removed what was left of the tattered silk leaf from the sticks and placed the remains on some clean white blotting paper. Although they were dirty they could not really be cleaned because of the gouache paintings which would have washed away.

4. The three vignettes were divided into three separate sections with tiny embroidery scissors which were exceptionally sharp.

5. Then we prepared three rectangles of Nylon Gossamer Fabric and some Cellofas paste.

6. Each separate piece of Gossamer was soaked in the Cellofas and then placed upon some clean white blotting paper. Then, with eyebrow tweezers, we placed each broken pleated scene onto the Gossamer. The scene was patted flat so that no pleats now showed, the edges were very gently pulled together so that no breaks could be seen either and then more Cellofas was applied on top.

Cellofas never stains; the stains come from one's own hands, so hands were washed in between every action JUST IN CASE. This meant we now had three scenes, each taken one at a time, which was soaked with Cellofas and backed with Gossamer, drying out. It was necessary in this case to place the *dry* silk onto the wet Gossamer, otherwise too much of the silk would have fluttered away – in this way it all bonded together with the second coat of Cellofas on top.

7. Whilst this was being done another craftsman was cleaning and mending the guard and the sticks properly – in just the way written in the last chapter. When they were finished they looked perfect and one could not see where the mend had been in any of the cases in point.

8. Another craftsman then tackled the replacement of a new leaf upon the old sticks which were ready, and black Chantilly was chosen for the job. This new Chantilly was a fortunate purchase from Allan's of Duke Street some time before, but even so, as the fabric was new we had to wash it to take out some surplus dressing which was making it too stiff. In time, working from the directions above, the Chantilly was placed upon the mother-of-pearl sticks with invisible threads, using two short fine needles, working always from the centre outwards; at one stage it seemed necessary to use four needles so that the tension was kept completely even.

9. Then we took the old cream lace "frames" which were now clean and dry and applied them onto the new Chantilly. First they were tacked into place, then, with a strong magnifying glass and small needles and invisible thread, we sewed the lace in place with tiny stitches about one eighth of an inch apart.

This took even more days than taking the lace apart in the beginning; the outline of the lace was very rococo, the design very intricate, so that each tiny flower or leaf had to be stitched all around. Equally we had to work all three at the same time in order to keep that tension accurate, otherwise the lace would have gone skew-eyed across the sticks very soon.

In the end we had three cream lace "frames" applied onto black Chantilly with some of the tiny flowers and leaves which had come adrift in the parcel sewn into the centres of the "frames"; this black Chantilly was applied onto creamy mother-of-pearl sticks and guards – and a final touch was added of some very fine hanging ribbons.

10. In the meanwhile the original painted scenes on silk had dried successfully onto their backgrounds of Nylon Gossamer Fabric. So then another craftsman cut around each scene, which happened to have

rather pleasing rococo rainceaux, leaving this curly and uneven edge to each. Then, with Cellofas paste again, the scenes were pasted onto three areas of contrasting velvet – a type of elephant-grey velvet, for that colour appeared once or twice in each picture. Once this was dry, the outlines of the creamy silk scenes were painted with two forms of gold-leaf paint to give them texture and depth against the grey behind, and then finally each scene was put into a Hogarth frame.

Now our lady owner had three pictures (which was what she liked best about the fan anyway) and a new fan of lace on her old sticks.

Some firm principles emerge from this experience. A great deal of fan restoration involves pure experimental work. There are so many types of fans that one can only give general guidance. Secondly there is immense value in writing down every step and stage of the way you have dealt with your fan. Such a record is bound to be invaluable at a later date when you have forgotten how you did some job originally; equally one learns so much from one's mistakes. Ideally you should have a friend to share your "trade secrets" with, it cuts the time you experiment by half and there is always one "other thing" you can add for each other in the way of advice.

How to pack a fan into a parcel

It is absolutely useless to accuse the postal authorities of damaging your fan in the parcel post. If it *is* damaged the responsibility lies squarely on your own shoulders. Here is some advice on packing a fan:-

1. Attach your own name, address and catalogue number to the fan, using a tie-on label and never pressure-sensitive adhesive tapes.

2. Wrap the fan carefully in clean white linen or cotton. Should any bad knocks in transit dislodge anything such as mother-of-pearl chips or sequins then the material keeps it in with the fan. Small items are easily lost in the folds of tissue paper when being unpacked. This is one occasion to put your wrapped fan into a plastic bag just in case of damp; especially around Christmas time the odd bottle of whisky gets smashed in the post and the last thing you want is a whisky-soaked fan.

3. Obtain a strong, rigid carton about twice the size and length of the fan itself. Never use its own original box; it would be far too old, delicate, easy to break and needless to send even if it seems suitable.

4. Take a length of *clean*, new tissue paper and, working from one corner, loosely roll it up like a giant cigar, leaving lots of air inside. Then tie the roll to look a little like a bird's nest. Make a couple of dozen of these "nests". This is how the Victoria and Albert Museum pack all their precious objects to travel world-wide.

5. Line the container with "nests" and settle the fan in the middle. The scheme is to cushion the fan with the trapped air in the tissue paper, but, even so, it must be firmly in place as well – so pack in as many nests as possible without jamming everything in tight.

6. Cover the box with corrugated paper.

7. Cover that with strong brown paper.

8. Hold together with gumstrip.

9. Address to the sender at least twice (once only for the United States Mail – this is a regulation).

10. Cover in at least four places with self-adhesive tape.

11. Insure it at the Post Office.

12. Write a covering note to the sender to say it is on its way, so if they are out they can make sure the parcel does not go astray. You can also take out what is known as "Compensation factors" with the Post Office.

Tissue-paper packing "nests"

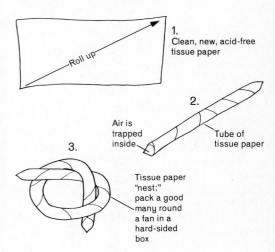

1. Clean, new, acid-free tissue paper

2. Tube of tissue paper
Air is trapped inside

3. Tissue paper "nest;" pack a good many round a fan in a hard-sided box

Display cases for fans

If your fan is in a display case:

1. Never put it in direct sunlight.

2. Never hang it over a radiator.

3. Take care with spotlights; electric lights can burn or fade so you would be best advised to shield any fluorescent tube with a Morden fluorescent tube jacket – see above in the section on repair suppliers.

4. Place a small bag of Silica Gel at a corner of the case so that you can control any damp.

If you want to display your fans in cases round your rooms and you cannot afford about a hundred pounds for each shaped case, you may care to make your own. You should realise, however, that you are reducing your fans' saleability by exposing them to light all the time and not allowing them to be pleated. If you have fans for fun or pleasure, however, rather than as an investment, you may easily care to look at them as you would look at a picture. This is how you can go about displaying them:

Right. *A collection of unusual fans.*
Top left: *"Dagger" fan of waxed calico set into a metal holder, together with its sheath of suede and cast metal.*
Top right: *Black silk fan sewn with gold and silver sequins and spangles, attached to a small pair of opera-glasses, produced by Asprey of Bond Street, London.*
Centre and bottom: *Austrian leather brisé fan with a painted coat of arms in the centre, the guardsticks with enamelled initials and an enamelled crown. The fan comes with its own matching leather case, blue-satin lined. All 19th century.*

1. Buy some old painting at an auction sale of the correct dimensions and of which you like the frame. Do remember to give about four inches *minimum* of space around the fan, especially if the frame is heavy. Measure your area before you go to the sale and measure any suitable pictures once you are there for the viewing. It is important to have a frame which would suit both your room and the fan.

2. Arrange a work-space which can be left severely alone for several days, because this will take up quite some room and you cannot do it all in one day.

3. Select your background material for lining the frame, such as velvet or watered silk etc. Use a contrast of surfaces; shiny material behind a matt-surfaced fan and vice versa, remembering that much depends on the colour and the material showing through the sticks without swamping them.

4. Always buy sufficient material to cover the backboard of the frame and line the inside of the frame from glass to backboard. This latter just might have to be put "on the cross" so give yourself plenty of leeway. Sometimes it is necessary, with old frames, to put in a liner first to cover any loose splinters and/or the additions to the frame to deepen it. Paint all the wood with Mystox LPL first.

5. See whether the frame is deep enough to accommodate the rivet. If not, you will have to fix wooden strips to the back of the frame and then screw them in place with brass screws.

6. Make your stand for your rivet end of the fan. This section of a fan can be in so many different shapes that no-one could provide fan stands to order; some are pointed, some rounded, some have tassels or ribbons so your fan stand will have to be custom made. You can shape plastic in heat, carve wood, use small display stands for porcelain – the choice is up to you. I have even seen a small v-shaped fabric-covered pincushion filled with foam rubber which was most effective.

7. With an adhesive such as Copydex line

Top left. *Neapolitan fan. Late 18th century. Obverse showing Vesuvius erupting, the inscription being 'Eruzione'. The sticks are of pierced ivory and cut-steels spangles.*

Centre left. *Reverse of the above fan showing visitors at Pompeii, and the inscription 'Tempo Isdea'. The barrel rivet has amethyst finials.*

Bottom left. *"Imperceptible Fan" of a printed and hand-coloured paper leaf and silvered bone sticks, the guardstick of mother-of-pearl. 1828.*

Top right. *Advertising fan for the opening of the Roof Garden, Hotel Meurice. c. 1910.*

Centre right. *18th century English fan with three vignettes of people in landscapes and two flower studies. The paper leaf is decoupé and punched at the top and has tiny gold leaves and spangles applied. The sticks are of pierced ivory. c. 1760.*

Bottom right. *Japanese Nanga fan painted by Hine Taizan (1813-69). Landscape: temple on the wooded slopes of a hill. Ink and touches of colour on gold-sprinkled paper. Inscription: "Learning from Shen Shih-t'ien's 'Fresh snow over the Mountains'; Taizan-jin". Seals: 'Shonen'; Cho-?roku'.*

Overleaf. *French fan c. 1840. Printed and hand-coloured, together with mother-of-pearl carved and gilded sticks.*

the inside of your fan case, all around, from the glass to the backboard very neatly; first making sure that the glass in the frame is not going to fall forwards when the fan is in its case. See that the grain of the fabric is all going the same way and that no ragged edges can be seen from the front. Then clean the glass of the frame, both back and front, with the greatest care. There is nothing more depressing than getting everything in place only to find there are unaccountable smears on the glass and you have to start again.

8. Press your fabric for the back of the frame – steam velvet – and allow an overlap of at least two inches which will be cut away afterwards. You must position the fan carefully in the frame so that this fabric can be seen and the fan is not virtually jammed up against the frame.

9. Apply your fabric to the top one and a half inches of the board with either Copydex or a PVA adhesive, following the directions carefully. Allow to dry for at least twenty-four hours. Some people make ventilation holes in the case, but this could allow entry for tiny insects. Such ventilation holes should be covered with Nylon Gossamer Fabric, painted with Mystox solution. A small bag of Silica Gel in the corner of the frame will control any internal dampness.

10. Fix your fan onto the backboard fabric. Firstly you have to position it in place with non-rusting pins. Then you have to make up your mind if the balance is correct for you. One guard will show and there may be a tassel or ribbons, so you will have to fiddle around with it patiently until you are completely satisfied.

Then sew the sticks to the fabric (which is loose as it has not yet been stuck down) with invisible clear nylon thread. Always start in the centre and work outwards, using two needles and not removing the pins until after you have finished. Work as close to the leaf as possible and work slowly; endlessly wash your hands.

If necessary hold the guards apart at the back with a tiny piece of split cane as guards are liable to spring together. You could also use a sheet of shaped clear perspex.

To hold the fan against the fabric-covered backboard you can use a tiny, clear nylon rod; warm it, bend to shape, cut off a suitable length, make a hole in its base and screw into position with minute brass screws.

Leave for twenty-four hours at least. When you are quite satisfied that everything is perfect then you can continue…but it is amazing how often folds suddenly appear the next day because the tension of your stitches is slightly uneven.

You must rest the backboard almost upright for twenty-four hours as a trial, it is no good leaving it flat on a table.

Once you are completely satisfied – and there is no going back after the next stage, you can lightly stick the remainder of the fabric, complete with the fan, onto the backboard. Do not soak the material as you don't want any adhesive to come through to your own fan. If you have made a mistake or wish to change the colour of your fabric at a later date, the fan must be able to be lifted straight out without any damage.

11. Fix the backboard onto the frame. Hold it upright BUT NOT ON ITS FACE or the fan is going to slip off its shaped stand and you are back where you were. Use non-rusting screws, never tacks or nails, which safely go right through your wooden additions to your frame. Then cut away any surplus fabric hanging out. Neaten with gumstrip over the joints.

12. Fit new nylon cord from two rings on the sides of the frame to hang. The whole frame plus fan is now really quite heavy so it is best to have the rings set into the wooden frame rather than onto the backboard. Some people like to add a rouleau of matching fabric to cover the cord and then suspend it, as they did in the eighteenth century, from two places on the picture rail; but never use ribbon or fabric *without* the cord inside.

Every now and again an act of extraordinary generosity comes one's way, and a most significant one happened recently.

My friend Miss Esther Oldham, the American Patron of the Fan Circle, was once the student of Mr De Witt Clinton Cohen of New York, Florence and Paris, the most knowledgeable person on the subject of fans during his life in America. His wife was the founder of the famous Needle and Bobbin Club of New York and renowned for her Museum Lace Collection.

Top left. *A fan that was possibly made for the vineyard, showing "Nuba Fabrica para Remozar Viejas" (or "a new factory to rejuvenate the elderly"). Once having gone through the machine of wine the old crone (left) is young enough to marry again (right). Hand-painted paper with ivory sticks. Spanish. c. 1780.*
Bottom left. *Painted Viennese ivory brisé fan. c. 1860.*
Overleaf. *A very large fan made from 'lace-bark' of the lagetta lintearia tree. The fan is basically made from lace-bark, bordered by 'spatha', the sheath of the fruit of the mountain cabbage palm, the sticks and guards of tortoiseshell, the tassel made from the fibre of the pineapple plant. The decoration consists of dried, pressed ferns. Made either in Jamaica or Indonesia. c. 1870.*

Originally the famous "Beggar's Opera Fan" belonged to Mr De Witt Clinton Cohen, and he earnestly implored Miss Oldham to research it thoroughly, as there were, at that time, only three of these fans in the world. This is the only one with bars of music from the opera painted upon the guardsticks. (Since then it has transpired that five are known, one selling at Christies in London in 1978 for $4,200.)

Miss Oldham eventually became the owner of the fan herself and she spent the better part of ten years on research on the subject; now, rather than let the work be lost to the fan world, she has allowed me to insert it in this book.

The "Mask Fan" was made in England in 1728 and first appeared at the Beggar's Opera there, soon reaching Spain and America. Apparently this one was either especially executed for the Spanish market or for one particular Spanish person, and has been referred to by both MacIver Percival and Wooliscroft Rhead in their respective books.

My very grateful thanks to a most erudite and gracious lady.

THE MYSTERY OF A "CURIOUS" FAN
A Mask Fan
By Esther Oldham

The most unusual and sensational fan of the early eighteenth century was the "curious" mask fan which was advertised in London and in the Boston News Letter of August 8–15, 1728 which ran as follows:

"George Harding, lately from London, now at John Pitts, Confectioner in Cornhill, Boston, mounteth all sorts of fans as well as any done in Old England. He likewise hath an assortment of 'curious' mounts which he will dispose of very reasonably not proposing to stay long in these parts." (Figure I).

It is interesting to note here that on January 26, 1728, the first performance of the *Beggar's Opera* was produced in London.

Probably no Opera of the eighteenth century created more of a furore and excitement among the musical elite of the world than did the *Beggar's Opera*, so political was its content, so charming its tunes, and so different its structure, omitting, as it did, the usual Prologue and Epilogue.

John Gay, poet and dramatist, was an accomplished flautist. In one advertisement, "The songs of the Beggar's Opera" were transposed for the flute containing more than sixty airs printed by John Watts at the Printing Office in Wild Court (Tottenham Court) Lincoln's Inn Fields, price 2s.6d."

One advertisement that appeared during the production of the Opera said, "A new and entertaining fan, consisting of fourteen of the most favorite songs taken out of the Beggar's Opera, with the musick in proper keys within the compass of the flute, curiously engraved on a copper plate. Sold for the author at Gay's head, in Tavistock St."

We note that, on the left-hand side of the fan, on the Mask Fan, a customer is trying out the music on the flute in the Music and Print Shop, perhaps in John Watt's Printing Shop in Tottenham Court. Another customer plucks the strings of a lute.

Lincoln's Inn Fields, situated on Portugal Street, was sometimes referred to as "Portugal Row", probably in honour of

Charles II and his Queen who was the Infanta of the King of Portugal, Catherine of Braganza.

The great manor houses of the time were built in the spacious country fields on the fringes of London. Being Portuguese, the Queen brought with her Portuguese attendants, as well as many Oriental curiosities which became fashionable fads, among which were Chinese fans.

An advertisement in the *Daily Journal*, February 1, 1728 stated, "On Monday at Lincoln's Inn Fields Theatre, as well as last night, there was a prodigious concourse of Nobility and Gentry present at the Beggar's Opera. No theatrical performance for many years has met with so much applause."

King George II and his Court attended eleven performances.

John Rich, the producer of the *Beggar's Opera* was a born showman while John Gay, the Author, was fascinated with Beggars, and in his poetic way, he likened himself to one; thus Hogarth placed the Beggar in the centre of the fan leaf.

Omitting the usual Prologue and Epilogue to the Opera, Gay wrote instead, a short Dialogue between a Beggar (played by Mr Chapman) and a Player in the Opera, (a Mr Milwood); the Beggar giving his (Gay's) reasons to the audience for writing the Opera. It was an astonishing departure and novel experiment which caught the fancy of the musical world.

On the fan leaf we see the Beggar holding a News Sheet as the central character advertising the Opera.

Situated, as the theatre was, on the outskirts of London, the region was infested with pick-pockets, robbers, highwaymen, and was overrun with Beggars.

John Gay writes of the wilderness in 1716 in *"Trivia"* or *"The Art of Walking in the Streets of London."* He draws a vivid picture:

"Where Lincoln's INN's wide space, is railed around,
Cross not with vent'rous step there oft is found the luring thief,
Who while the daylight shone,
Made the walls echo with his Beggar's tone etc…"

We note also in *"Trivia"* there were no sidewalks at that period but simply a series of sturdy wooden posts separating pedestrians along the cobblestone roads from the carriages and traffic.

On the right-hand side of the fan leaf we find seven "Sturdy Posts" in a row as described by Gay – in front of the buildings.

The large building with small dormer windows in the background of the fan, represents Lincoln's Inn Fields Theatre, while the Music and Print Shop of John Watt was probably located within the building (Tottenham Court). Hogarth was topographical in the minutest details of his drawings.

The Beggar's News Sheet has the following words in Spanish *"El Diario De Hoy,"* a Spanish paper *"The Daily Journal,"* corresponding to the English newspaper.

On the left-hand side of the fan leaf we notice an enraged couple from whom issue balloon-like ribbons with the Spanish words "Gueramino" (bad man) and "Este Enojaris"

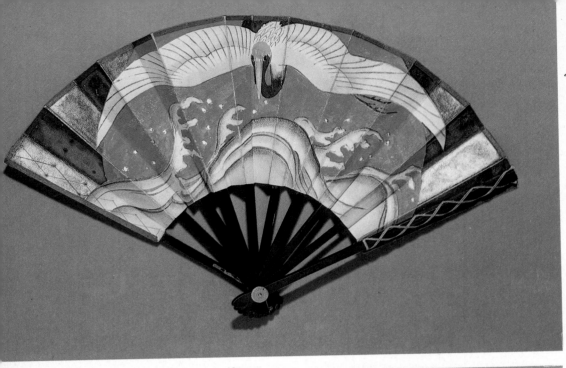

(the angry one). Hogarth was the first artist ever to portray Comedy on fans.

In the original Opera, Scene IX, Lucy Lockit, who was in love with the elegant Highwayman, MacHeath, but was wronged by him, cries out – "You baseman, you, how can you look me in the face after what hath past between us! Oh MacHeath, thou hast robbed me of my quiet etc...to see thee tortured would give me pleasure." Lucy Lockit is seen striking at MacHeath with her broom in desperate anger, and continues her violent tirade with the words, "Tis the pleasure of all you fine men to insult the women you have ruined."

Hogarth loved the humorous side of life, and took pleasure, no doubt, in still another sketch he made for the *Beggar's Opera* in which all the characters were burlesqued, wearing animal heads. (Figure II).

He made at least five or six different drawings and sketches of the *Beggar's Opera*, both for fans and hand-screens.

It is believed he drew the scene in Newgate Prison with MacHeath on trial, directly from the Prison, itself. (Figure III).

All of Hogarth's engravings were made in two sizes, consequently they were readily mounted on fans.

Probably no one did more to publicize the Opera than Hogarth and his fans. They were found in everyone's hands in England, Spain and America. The French were slow to "Catch on" as they disapproved of the Morality of MacHeath, the Highwayman.

Hogarth repeatedly admonished the Public to – "Watch the newspapers for his engravings, and particularly his FANS." Fans at that period were as important as a News Media as were newspapers, themselves. He advertised in the *"Daily Journal," "The Country Journal," "The Craftsman," "The Daily Advertiser," "The Daily Post"* etc....

His fans and engravings were also extensively advertised in the newspapers in the American Colonies from Georgia to Massachusetts as early as 1728.

The Mask fans were engraved or etched in brown ink and hand coloured.

While the Beggar on the fan leaf holds the centre of the stage, the lady proceeding towards him with upraised full-faced mask, represents the all conquering Polly Peacham, the Heroine of the Opera, played by the noted actress, Lavinia Fenton.

Top left. *Japanese fan. A great crane with outspread wings spanning the leaf, planing above a red sun, mountains and sea. Black ebony sticks and guards sewn to the leaf with a criss-cross of corded thread; large gilt pivot. 19th century.*
Centre left. *A modern Chinese rigid, or screen fan, painted on silk.*
Bottom left. *A mock-rococo English fan, delicately painted on silk. The sticks are of bone, impressed with some gilding. c. 1905.*
Top right. *A large Japanese fan of silvered paper, painted with sparrows. Wooden sticks and guard. c. 1890.*
Bottom right. *German fan dated 1738, the paper leaf painted with scenes from the life of a lady. Inscribed and dated. Ivory sticks painted with miniatures and guardsticks "enclouté".*

Polly Peacham was in love with, and secretly married to, the Highwayman MacHeath, a fact unknown to Lucy Lockitt.

In real life "Polly" was enamoured with a dashing Portuguese Nobleman, but later on, married Lord Bolton.

"It was possibly, as some recompense for its authors' (John Gay's) defence of their most powerful weapon, THE FAN, that the ladies helped to swell the tide of prosperity of The Beggar's Opera" according to the noted authority on Fans, G. Wolliscroft Rhead.

Quoting in part from Gay's imaginative and lengthy poem "The Fan" written in 1713, we became acquainted with the *Mask* or *Peeping fan of China* which Hogarth adopted:

THE FAN

"So shall the British fair their minds improve,
And on the FAN to climates rove,
Here China's ladies shall their pride display
etc.....
The PEEPING FAN in modern times shall
    rise,
Through which unseen the female ogle
    flies."

It is recorded these fans were sold at Mrs Vuljohn's in Cranbourn Alley, at Mr Gay's Head in Tavistock St., Mrs Jackson's at the 3 Fans, Mr Markham's at the 7 Stars in Fleet St., at Mrs Robotham's in Pope's Head Alley, and at John Watt's in Tottenham Court (Wild Court).

Hogarth established his own engraving shop at Ye Golden Ball at the corner of Cranbourn Alley in 1720. He was apprenticed to the greatest of all fan engravers, Mr Ellis Gamble.

He made Trade Cards, and Theatre Benefit Tickets for the Players in the *Beggar's Opera*. He was closely associated with John Gay and John Rich who held him in high esteem.

One Trade Card is particularly interesting as it was made for Hogarth's sisters; Mary and Ann Hogarth's "FROCK SHOP" located in Ye King's Arms in Tottenham Court, across the courtyard from Lincoln's Inn Fields Theatre. (Figure IV).

Without question, Hogarth's mask fans would have been sold there as an accessory to their "Frocks".

Overleaf top. *Chinese fan showing people in a landscape. Red lacquered and gilded sticks and guard. c. 1780.*
Bottom. *Canton "Fan of a Thousand Faces." c. 1840. The face of each individual is made from a sliver of ivory stuck onto the design. The sticks and guards are of lacquered papier-maché. These fans were for export only.*

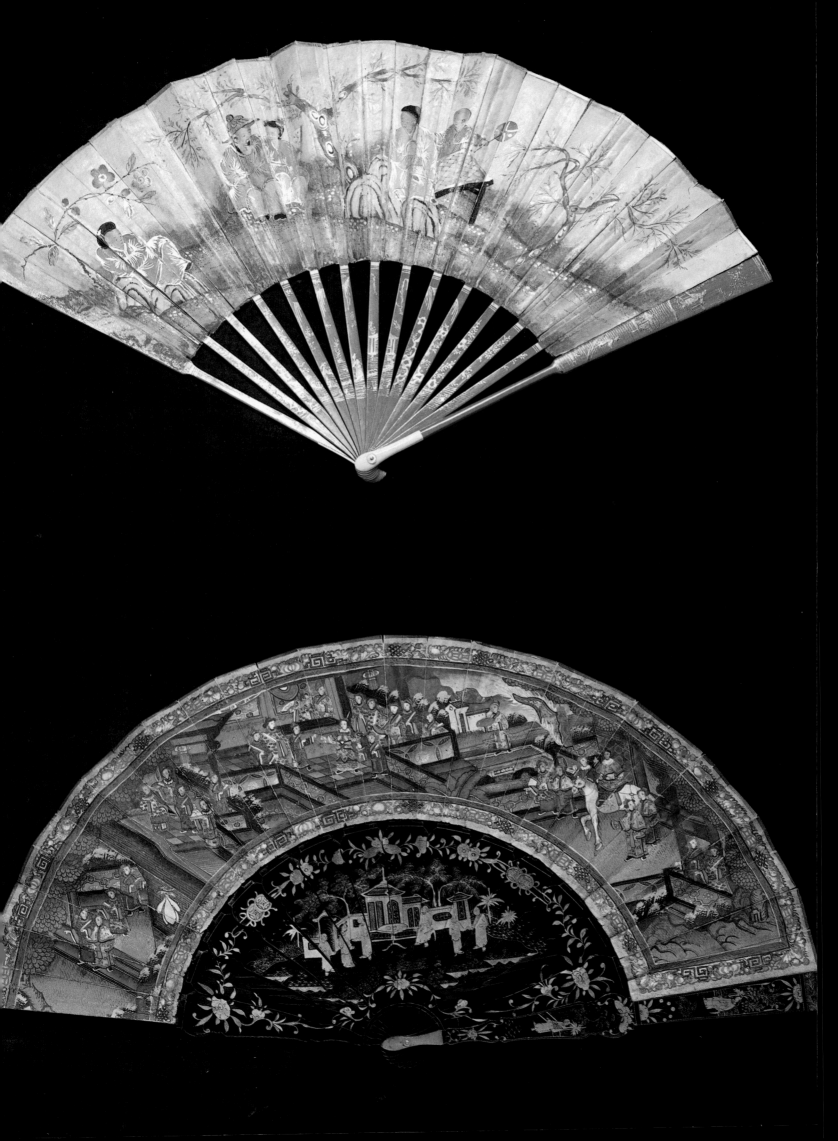

Hogarth owed much to his patroness, the Duchess of Queensberry, for whom he acted as secretary at one time, and was familiar with her pet monkey which was the favourite house-pet in fashionable London, so it was not surprising to find a monkey playing a violin on his mask fan. "Singerie" was the order of the day at that era. In Figure V, Hogarth combines the pet monkey, and the full-faced mask on the dressing table of an elegant lady.

Lincoln's Inn Fields was a mecca for the wealthy Spanish visitors and there was a Coffee House called "The Spaniard" to accommodate their taste.

Perhaps, too, some of the mask fans were made to suit the fancy of the Spanish tourist, the wording on the fans being inscribed in Spanish rather than in English.

Examining Figure I closely we see an inscription on the top left-hand side of the fan written in Portuguese which reads:

Al Señor, Dn
Matheo Juille g:DE
Dios M ann
Sevilla

Which freely translated says, "To the distinguished Don Matheo Juille, May God preserve you for many years. Seville."

As the *Beggar's Opera* was performed in Seville, Spain, in 1729, it is probable many mask fans were exported there. Seville was the centre of the arts, at that period.

The pierced ivory fan sticks are also intriguing, being well painted with Moorish towers, insects, castanets, and small fruits, such as, strawberries and cherries, both of which were among the Hawker's wares in the Street Cries of London in Hogarth's time.

Top right. *The Beggar's Opera fan, burlesqued by William Hogarth, made for John Gay's opera.*
Bottom right. *William Hogarth's painting, showing MacHeath, the highwayman, on trial in jail. Tate Gallery, London.*
Below. *Mary and Ann Hogarth's trade card for their "Frock Shop" in Ye King's Arms, made by Hogarth for his sisters. (From Lady Charlotte Schreiber's "Fans and Fan Leaves".)*

FIG. 8. "FROCK SHOP" KEPT BY MARY AND ANN HOGARTH
A proof impression. An engraving by T. Cook, from a drawing by Hogarth
Published by Longman, Hurst & Rees, January, 1807

The guard-sticks carry out the Musical theme with musical instruments and sheet music painted on them.

The success of this brilliant Opera was well known in the British Colonies of America.

The earliest newspaper notice of a Theatre in New York occurs in 1733 when "George Talbot sold furniture next door to the Playhouse." The *Beggar's Opera* had travelled far and wide.

It is recorded that Mr Kean of London was manager of a Company of Players who performed the *Beggar's Opera* in London January 14, 1731 which soon afterwards came to America. Mr Kean was described as "A gentleman lately from London."

A Ballard Opera called *Flora* with a libretto by Hippesley (who played Mr Peacham in Gay's *Beggar's Opera*) was played in South Carolina in 1735, thus it is believed that the *Beggar's Opera*, acclaimed by the musical elite of the world as the greatest Opera of the time, may well have appeared in fashionable New York in 1733.

Left. *18th century Mask fan made for the Beggar's Opera, 1728, from Hogarth's design. Oldham collection, Museum of Fine Arts, Boston, U.S.A.*

Because shellac comes from a combination of the exudation from certain trees in India and the East, together with the secretion deposited on them by an almost innumerable amount of shell lice. The mixture of the two produces shellac as a resin, which had been traded to Persians, Arabs and Turks for centuries before it made its way into Europe.

Top. *Black Chantilly lace fan. c. 1880. The sticks of blonde tortoiseshell with the name "Aline" in gold and diamonds on the guardstick. French.*
Left. *Asymmetrical fan of eagles' feathers, the whole half-wing mounted on tortoiseshell, with a silver initial on the guard. Possibly Austrian. c. 1900.*
Above. *Brazilian humming-bird fans; one has an arrangement of feathers on a turned ivory handle – even incorporating an iridescent beetle. The other is of scarlet and white feathers and a minute humming-bird perched within maribou. c. 1870.*
Right. *Female ostrich feather fan, mounted on tortoiseshell sticks, with a pierced, modelled and enamelled section on the guardstick, possibly made in Russia, with cabochon gemstones. c. 1890.*
Overleaf. *Chantilly lace applied to smoked mother-of-pearl sticks and guards. c. 1860. From M. Duvelleroy's own collection.*

copied from the Indians); the French called it all *vernis de la chine* or *lacquinage* and in Germany it was termed *Indianish werk*.

On what was japanning applied? To begin with it was wood, then it might be on thin iron on tinware and finally on papier-maché. The technique was to cover the wood with fine muslin, followed by an application of gesso – a composition of chalk and parchment size, applied in successive thin coats to the surface. When hardened this could be recarved, sanded, punched and/or gilded. The object was then painted with their own types of japanning, and, in certain ways, this influenced Continental workers who saw a solid future for themselves by developing their own techniques.

These japanners of furniture, boxes, trunks, screens, looking-glasses and clockcases were all influencing each other in Northern Europe. They adapted to several economic aspects of contemporary life: the lack of wood for large furniture (especially in England after the Great Fire of 1666) meant that there was a need – which became a fashion – for japanning; caning for chair seats, and *really* stretching woods through marquetry and parquetry.

The interest in the Orient multiplied because of the variety of Dutch imports and one of the quirks of fashion was to have one's walls hung with decorated leather. Around the time of the Restoration there was great interest in leather screens (some japanned as well) in the style of Spain and the Netherlands and the technique extended to applying the leather onto battens attached to the walls of a room.

One Hugh Robinson, trained in Amsterdam, announced that he would produce leather "brighter than gold" and in 1716 the *London Gazette* carried an advertisement from a leather gilder, Joseph Fletcher, who produced "leather hangings in the latest fashion of the Chinese style to cover walls, settees and screene."

Most people believed in the seventeenth century that shellac was the basis for Oriental lacquer (the confusion is ably sorted out in gradual stages in Dr Huth's book) and it was not until between 1690 and 1700 that Father Filippo Bonanni, under the patronage of Cosimo, Grand Duke of Tuscany, published an accurate report on Chinese lacquer and explained that the *Tsi* tree could neither be shipped to Europe nor could it be cultivated in the Western hemisphere. He suggested certain substitutes, which most people had been using anyway in their own recipes, and craftsmen happily continued to imitate Oriental lacquer in the way in which is now generally termed japanning.

Japanning

On the whole, in the Western world, shellac was mixed with spirits of wine, used as a thinner, and combined with a siccative or catalyst (litharge cobalt or manganese). There were, according to Dr Huth, other resins which were also considered such as copal, sandarach, sanguinis draconis, pix greca and amber – which was also called either bernstein, agtstein or succinic. What

was missing throughout were the tiny quantities of *Tsi* resin which gives the lustre and durability to Oriental work.

European japanning was a substitute for Oriental lacquer and developed as a technique quite separately; partly because the ingredients of true lacquer were simply not available and partly because the recipes, when they could avail themselves of them, were almost totally incomprehensible. So Westerners used varnish, the next best thing, and with which they had been familiar for centuries – called either *vernis, fernis* or *firnis*.

Varnish was used in the seventeenth and eighteenth centuries as a solution made of an oil combined with a hardening and drying ingredient, today called a siccative. The application of several coats of varnish, clear or pigmented, gave an object something of the appearance of having been lacquered in the Oriental manner.

In the seventeenth century the Dutch, the greatest traders of their era, especially to the Orient, lumped all Oriental lacquer and European imitations into the same word *lacwerk;* the English called imitations *Japan work* (although they thought much of it was

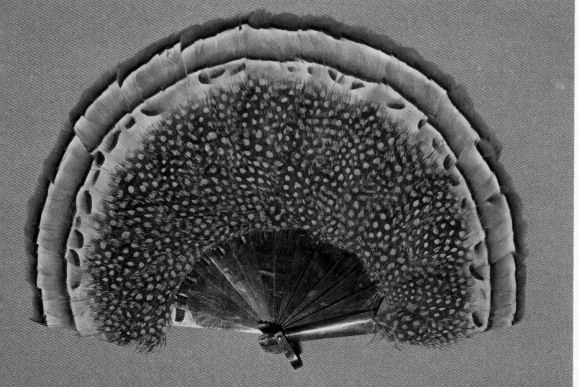

Top left. *18th century Dutch(?) fan. c. 1750. The central motif, in a medallion, shows a man playing the flute, a girl with a tambourine and a seated lady playing the violin. The pale grey background has a "semis" of stars and flowers, together with a lace ribbon, painted in gouache. The carved ivory sticks are painted with a floral decoration and a motif of lace.*

Left. *Feather fan, made up of grouse, pheasant and other feathers, with simulated tortoiseshell sticks. 19th century.*

Top right. *Antique lace and contemporary appliquéd embroidery on the leaf, showing a ship shape with a lady, putti and flowers painted in gouache and signed 'M. Rodriguez'. c. 1880-90. French. The sticks are of blonde tortoiseshell with initials in gold on the guard.*

Bottom right. *English 18th century fan, the paper leaf painted with an allegorical scene of four ladies representing the four seasons, and their attributes, in a classical landscape. Intricately carved ivory sticks and guards, the sticks carved with dancing figures – ladies and gentlemen. The pivot and handle are later additions.*

Someone who actively encouraged the style at the turn of the century was King William of Orange who, when crowned King of England, had half of the Tudor Hampton Court Palace torn down to attempt an updating in style, employing Sir Christopher Wren to remodel the King's and Queen's State Apartments. These were then refurnished with a mixture of Dutch and English furniture, Oriental ceramics and brilliant carvings of the bounties of Nature by Grinling Gibbons.

In an old account one reads that the King's State Drawing-Room was to be hung with "85 pieces of gilt leather cost at five shillings the piece", which must have made an impressive setting. Although the leather in the State Drawing Room is not visible today there is another fine room in that style, untouched, not far away at Ham House, near Richmond in Surrey, decorated in the 1680's by the immensely rich Duke and Duchess of Lauderdale.

Cured and treated calf or goat's skin was used; it is pointless to go into the techniques of leather wall-hangings here but I feel that, as so many workers were employed in this fashion at the time, it must have influenced the fan makers. This was, after all, when vellum fans were most in vogue and brought to a pitch of fineness which could have been no accident. Equally, I feel that, as with so many of the crafts in miniature, the makers of japanned fan sticks with vellum mounts were sensibly using the left-overs from other, larger objects such as japanned furniture and leather wall-hangings.

During the seventeenth century the parchment and vellum makers used similar techniques throughout of stretching each animal's skin (vellum is strictly calf-skin) previously soaked in a solution of lime, on a frame. Then they would "flesh" it (scrape) with blunt semi-circular knives until it was perfectly smooth. (These knives can be clearly seen in a seventeenth century seal of the Guild of the Prague parchment makers in the archives of the National Museum in Prague). Then they roughened the skin with a pumice-stone, rubbed in chalk and finally polished the surface.

An old recipe for first lubricating vellum so that it remained supple when pleated as a fan states: "Take 1 pound of Russian tallow; 6 ounces of beeswax; 4 ounces of black pitch; 3 pounds of common castor oil; ½ pound of soft paraffine; ½ ounce of citronella. Melt together in a saucepan, stirring occasionally, except for the citronella which you add when cool. Apply to the vellum."

Vellum was cheap enough and extremely hard-wearing; another form of leather was eventually used which has the generic term of "chicken-skin" today. This was the skin of an unborn kid, necessitating great expense as both animals were then killed, mother and child. Mr Martin Willcocks has done some research into this subject and has discovered that chicken-skin had been used by the Persians for a long time for tracing purposes. This obviously means that the skin is extremely fine and thin, it is semi-transparent and certainly translucent. If treated correctly it becomes a hard substance and it crackles when hit with snapped fingers. When used for fan leaves chicken-skin is usually two or three layers glued together. It seems probable that the treated skin was imported through Venice into Italy from Persia, for many an Italian fan is painted upon chicken-skin whereas in Northern Europe vellum was used far more because it was more viable economically.

Who, then, were the masters of japanning and varnishing in Europe – and where were the centres? One would naturally assume that they would work in guilds – but which? Would they join guilds of painters or cabinet-makers? In London, before 1695, there was the guild called "Patentees for lacquering after the manner of Japan", in Amsterdam they were called *verlakkers* and in Venice they were *depentores*. But sadly the various archives have hardly any information about their members; many were itinerant workers or dilettantes, happily and universally using Stalker and Parker's *A Treatise on Japanning and Varnishing*, which was published in London in 1688.

Centres of Japanning and Varnishing in Europe.

Incomparable Venice, magnetic city of the eighteenth century, was a famous centre for all manner of portable souvenirs bought by her cosmopolitan visitors. The first known japanned work there as a trade was c. 1660, well written up by the Huguenot traveller Misson by 1688 when he visited Venice. Father Coronelli (1650–1702) invented a special varnish for globes (its chief ingredient being sandarach) and for further details of the seventeenth century Italian varnishes please read *Le lacche Veneziane del Settecento* by Giulio Lorenzetti, published in Venice in 1938 and *Mobili Veneziani Laccati* by Giuseppe Morazzoni, published in Milan in 1954.

Just because so many objects were made for the visitor one finds strange and exotic small objets d'art, made in Venice, lying about in stately homes and palaces all over the world today. It seems that the wood that they used for their japanned work was *cirmolo*, a type of alpine fir tree. They also used mother-of-pearl inlay and painted styles which were mainly copied from England and Holland. Nowhere else is there much reference to inlay-work, so it is reasonable to suppose that japanned fan sticks with inlay-work could have been made in Venice.

Venetian japanners were at the height of their skills by the mid-eighteenth century and we know that in 1754 there were twenty-five "lacquermasters", with more than double that sum of workers in their workshops, and by 1773 the number of masters had risen to forty-nine. "Lacquer" was everywhere, even complete rooms in some of those delicious palazzi; the colours most favoured in sun-dappled Venice were celadon, light blue or yellow.

In view of the massive amount of furniture made, in addition to completely panelled rooms, together with pincushion containers, boxes, trays, candlesticks and toilet-sets – it must stand to reason that, as lacquered fans and fan sticks were so popular in Europe and trade depended a good deal on souvenirs for sale, many must have been made in Venice. In 1780 the turning-point came. Napoleon began to change the shape of Europe and japanning went out of fashion; work continued for a while spasmodically until the middle of the nineteenth century – but never with the bravura of the eighteenth.

Turin came second in importance as a centre for japanning in Italy. To get an idea of the quality of the work there one should visit the Royal Palace (decorated by Pietro Mass c.1735) or gaze upon some of the splendid furniture (c.1750) by Francesco Servorcelli at Stupingi.

Colour and grace came from Venice but the japanning of Genoa did not have the same finish. However the term *vernice della Madalena* must be mentioned here because it is a generic term in Italy, just like *vernis Martin* is in France. It developed because of a master in japanning who lived near the church of S. Madalena in Genoa – and by 1765 there were many recorded masters using his techniques and recipes.

Other centres in Italy (Rome, Modena etc) were not really interested in japanning at all, and any very grand house with artefacts made from lacquers or varnishes are known to have been imported.

Some masters worked in Hamburg in Germany, but the fashion was slow to spread. Musical instruments, such as clavichords, were made of wood and japanned (especially by the masters Fleischer, Zell or Hass, in their workshops) the exteriors being either red or green or gilt, and the interiors of paler and softer colours. In Bremen one reads that there was only one master recorded, Nicolaus Woltmann, c.1688 – having stated that he learnt his trade in England.

In Brunswick there was a French Huguenot master, Johann Christoph Lesieur, born in Hanover, and a citizen of Brunswick in 1717 – again working in the English style.

The most important and influential worker in japanning in Germany was Gerard Dagly of Berlin (possibly born in Spa) marvellously well-recorded in Berlin archives. Born c. 1665, he died in 1715; all his works are well written up, including the recipe for his varnish:

> 4 quarts *Spiritus Vini*
> 4 quarts *Gumma Lacca*
> 2 quarts *Gummi Sandarac*
> 4 lots *Sanguis Draconis*

There are a great many books on German japanning and I would therefore refer you to Dr Huth's bibliography. These books list other masters such as Andreas Volkert (active c.1708–33) and David Mennewitz (who also worked in Meissen and was in association with Dresden leatherworkers).

Dresden and Meissen were big centres as well for japanning and varnishing and many an itinerant worker would go to decorate various sumptuous palaces or great houses in Bavaria, Baden, Hesse, Wurtenberg etc. Especially outstanding was the work seen in both Munich and Vienna during the eighteenth century.

Right. *A selection of tiny fans, the smallest being of silver or gold for charm bracelets. None of them is over two inches in height. Various periods from 1800 to the present day.*
Overleaf. *Japanned European Brisé fan; highly coloured, showing an amateur theatrical performance of a 'classical' play. Late 17th century Dutch.*

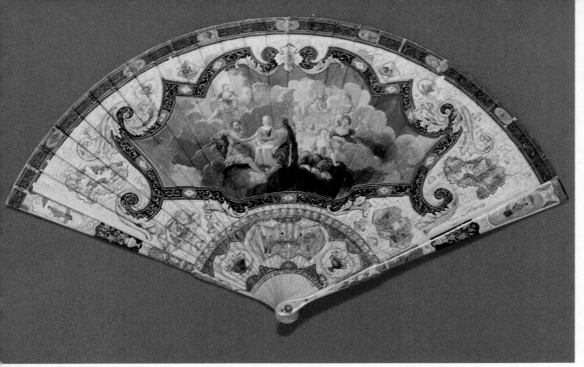

It must surely follow that, as so many workers were employed in the creation of japanned and varnished furniture, boxes, carriages and so on that they would prefer to make their own fans and fan sticks, rather than import them from another country.

So what about the famous French japanners?

Louis XIV, Cardinal Richelieu and Cardinal Mazarin were perhaps the leading collectors of as many items imported from the Far East as they could lay their hands upon. Then the French workers began to copy the Oriental techniques to a certain extent (the earliest known objects are two cabinets at Versailles with "lacquer" panels dating from 1665) and within ten years there were masters working in the Royal workshops in Paris. Their work is well documented today, with dates and prices, and makes fascinating reading.

One significant worker was Jacques Dagly (b.1665 in Spa, d.1728 in Paris) who had been dismissed in Berlin (where he had been working with his brother) and became a master of the *Ouvrages de la Chine* shop at Les Gobelins in 1713. He patented his recipe, probably the one used in Berlin, with his brother Gerard, and took on two partners – both painters – Pierre de Neufmaison and Claude III Audran. Most important, however, from the point of view of fan collectors, was that an edict of that year gave him the right (for twenty years) to produce a lacquer with which to cover all kinds of pliable materials including silk, linen and leather, and to be used to protect furniture decorated in colour. Dagly's lacquer was called *vernis de Gobelins* and I feel there is a far better case for French fans to be called *vernis de Gobelins* than *vernis Martin*. His output was so fashionable and so important that when Peter the Great came to visit Paris in 1717 he was taken on a ceremonial visit to Dagly's workshops. He was eventually succeeded by Pierre de Neufmaison, and he by his son-in-law Charles André Tramblin – who worked for the King, worked for the Emperor in Vienna in 1761 and finally died in poverty in Russia.

Top left. *Very fine brisé jappaned fan, showing "The Banquet of the Gods". The white colouring is typical of the Martin brothers, but the fan is too early for their manufacture. It was probably made by craftsmen of the "Ouvrages de la Chine" shop at Les Gobelins. c. 1710–13.*
Centre left. *Japanned European Brisé fan, including contemporary shagreen box. This may be from the "Ouvrages de la Chine" shop at Les Gobelins, c. 1713, made by Jacques Dagly (b. 1665 in Spa, d. 1728 in Paris, having worked with his brother in Berlin). Very fine quality.*
Bottom left. *"Almanac Fan". c. 1750. Printed paper, with sticks of painted wood to look like Oriental lacquer.*
Top right. *French fan, "La Marchande D'Amours". Hand-coloured print on silk; silvered and gilded bone sticks, paste rivet. c. 1775. From M. Duvelleroy's own collection.*
Bottom right. *A lithographed, hand-coloured Spanish fan of the 19th century, with carved bone sticks. Made in the Philippines and partly silvered.*
Overleaf. *French, painted silk fan, with embroidery and sequins. Sticks of ivory, carved, pierced, silvered and gilded. c. 1775.*

Antoine Watteau was a japanner…from 1708 he joined Claude III Audran at the Palais du Luxembourg; various claims have been made that he worked in *vernis Martin* which is impossible, as they did not start making their varnish until well after Watteau was dead. But it shows how these rumours begin.

Only isolated snippets of knowledge are known about French japanning until after c.1730, when fuller records were kept during the reign of Louis XV.

Complete rooms were panelled in japanned work and wonderful furniture was made by the greatest ébénistes of all times. Black lacquer was in favour, in spite of the fact Louis XV hated the colour, and there was occasionally a type of work imitating aventuring stone, brownish-red in colour, which glitters as if gold particles were scattered on the surface. This is sometimes seen on really good French fans of the period and I feel that, as this technique was almost exclusively used in France on furniture etc, when seen on fans as well one can confidently say that they are French.

Another small reminder of the furniture makers and the maitres ciseleurs-fondeurs are the techniques of gilding on fans. As there were now so many elaborate gilt ormolu mounts by the Caffieris et al on furniture made by masters such as Van Reisenburgh, Jacques Dubois etc – the decoration on fans began to take on the same flavour, and similar styles of gilding were used to outline many a cartouche. One sees the typical cross-hatching of German masters and the rococo scrolls of the French and, just occasionally, a fan can be attributed to a country purely because of its gilding rather than its painted decoration.

The Martin family is legendary; they worked in two generations and in their most carefully documented records, which mention even the tiniest patchbox, there is not one fan mentioned. It is also important to mention that not one single member of the family ever signed an item they made.

The first generation was Guillaume (d.1749) Etienne-Simon (d.1770) Julien (d.1752) and Robert (1706–1765). In 1730 they acquired their first Royal patent to protect their lacquer, and by 1748 their workshops were appointed Manufacture Royale, with three shops in Paris, making some exquisite small objects and continuing right up to decorating entire rooms.

The colour mostly associated with the Martin family was white, often embellished with green. It is true that they made objects for Madame de Pompadour and also Queen Marie Leszczynska, so there is the faintest possibility that the claims for fans made for these Royal ladies might be correct. But why were they never recorded?

The second generation was Guillaume-Jean (b.1713) Etienne-Francois (d.1771) Jean Alexandre (1738–1823) and Antoine Nicolaus (b.1742). Jean Alexandre also served Frederick the Great from 1747–66, but the last half of the eighteenth century found japanned objects sadly unfashionable and Jean Martin gave up the business in 1787 aged forty-six.

The Martin family made everything one could imagine, from furniture and carriages to elegant snuff-boxes, and almost all of their varnishes were applied onto papier-maché: layer on layer of moulded paper glued together, polished, painted and varnished and deliciously light to carry.

Previous writers on fans during the late nineteenth and early twentieth centuries wrote enthusiastically about *vernis Martin* fans; yet japanners of the eighteenth century in Europe were neither accurately documented at that time nor was there reliable provenance about the makes of *"vernis Martin"* fans. I feel that the earlier authors on fans recalled that the most famous japanners were the Martin family and cheerfully put two and two together – which added up to a legend.

Japanners in the Netherlands copied original Oriental imports rather than developing a style of their own during the seventeenth century, purely because they had those originals to hand; otherwise they adapted from the Dutch still life paintings of imported flowers as a form of public relations work about their country's source of wealth. Early in the eighteenth century it became extremely difficult to tell Dutch work from English work, but at least there was a tremendous vogue in the country for anything even remotely Oriental…and they had better chances of bringing in the more refined ingredients for making varnishes from the East.

A strong influence in style in both the Netherlands and England was the Huguenot Daniel Marot, jack-of-all-trades and master of most of them, who had a finger in a great many artistic pies. Craftsmen wandered about between England, Holland and the Scandinavian countries to such an extent that no japanning seems to be indigenous to any one of these countries exclusively. Political ties between Denmark, Norway and Sweden were linked until 1814, and ties between Guilds and through friendships existed between Scandinavia and England. The Norwegian, Niels Lochstoer (1714–85) was trained in London, Niels Dahlin (d.1787) of Sweden was first apprenticed in Paris and French masters taught craftsmen in Russia; so, without signatures, of which there are virtually none, it is impossible to attribute any fan to any specific worker in varnishes.

Left. *Two mourning fans for a very Merry Widow. Both are in black chiffon, one with a painted decoration of violets around the inset lace, the other with bright blue spangles embroidery. In both cases the sticks were probably imported from Malaya. c. 1870.*

Where I feel there must have been one of the liveliest and most long-lived centres for japanned or varnished fans and fan sticks was in the town of Spa in Belgium. As Dr Huth points out, the development of the japanners "offers a most informative example of the transition of a craft into an industry, *if only on a minor scale*." It is this minor scale which sounds so important, for if, as in the case of Etienne Martin, who spent twelve hundred working days around 1748 decorating the *Oratoire* and the *Cabinet a niches* at Versailles for Queen Maria Leszczynska, would it be possible that he would then consider making a few sticks for a tiny fan? It seems so improbable – there was such a demand for the Martin family's work – but on the other hand it just *might* have been an inexpensive way to train an apprentice.

But Spa was one of the oldest centres of the japanning trade, which began there before 1600 and continues today. It is near Liège and is dominated by the French-speaking Walloons. It is also a watering place and was so famous as such that it has given its name to the generic term of watering places all over Europe (Cheltenham Spa etc). To assist the leisurely invalids taking the waters special decorated staves called *bourdons* were made (the earliest recorded was in 1600) and then japanned.

As time went by so the workers in colourful wooden sticks and staves turned their attention to dozens of other small personal items such as japanned bowls and brushes and even small bellows to blow away hair-powder. What is so significant about their decoration is that their motifs were taken from Dutch landscape paintings and some of those genre scenes in the style of Teniers. So many so-called *vernis Martin* fans have these "Dutch" scenes on them, yet could not possibly have been made in either Paris or Amsterdam because of the sheer lack of quality, so that it seems more than possible they were made as souvenirs in Spa – with the shape and style of a French fan and the decoration of a 'Dutch' painting.

The first written evidence about their techniques was by Edmond Nessel in 1689 (Traité des Eaux, Liège) and the most entertaining description of the multitude of fripperies bought by himself or his lady friends can be read up in *Les amusements de Spa* or *The gallantries of the Spaw in Germany* by Baron von Pollnitz, first written in 1729 and with an English second edition in 1737. He mentions "lacquered" chip-containers, watch-cases, canes, tobacco-boxes etc "which mimic Japan so exactly that it is difficult to tell the difference".

According to Dr Huth the workers in japanned ware in Spa used wood from either the plane tree, the alder or the linden. First the object was shaped, then soaked in water from the Pouhon spring, which was rich in tannin and defended the wood against wood-worm. There was no undercoating, which is essential in Chinese and Japanese lacquer, but the ground colours were solved in glue. Then the decoration was applied with gouache colours, the piece was "lacquered" with sandarac and polished a number of times. This again ties up with many so-called *vernis Martin* fans with so called Dutch designs, for it is more than obvious that no undercoating has been first applied beneath the general decoration – they are merely varnished pictures.

The workers at Spa were so prolific that they exported their varnished wares to other cities such as Aix-la-Chapelle (another watering-place with the same type of customers, often wealthy invalids who collected souvenirs to pass the time) and quite a few of their masters were asked to serve at various European courts during the eighteenth century. The first break in the craft came at the time of the French Revolution but, with several other hesitations, the workers at Spa are still putting out "lacquerwork" today.

Fate, over-production, changes in artistic styles and finally the French Revolution virtually killed the fashion for European japanned fans or fan sticks. Far better historians than I may feel that I have put too much emphasis upon the background of lacquer and japanning, the workers and their techniques in each country. But, as so little has been written on this subject until now I wanted to make the point to fan collectors that *each* country in Europe, was copying oriental techniques – but with their own recipes – during the seventeenth and eighteenth centuries, and not France alone.

I also feel that dating of fans should be re-examined, some japanned ones may be earlier than originally listed; that *vernis Martin* should no longer be used as a generic term; that collectors should consider whether their japanned fans might be made in Venice or Berlin or Spa as well as Paris and, finally, that the words japanned or varnished (for European fans) and lacquered (for Oriental fans) should be substituted in future works by fan historians and present-day collectors.

The Fan Circle

THE FAN CIRCLE is a society for anyone interested in fans, whether as a collector, a member of Museum staff, an Art Historian, a person interested in or associated with Western European dress or an Orientalist. THE FAN CIRCLE was formed in 1975. The spur was a sudden interest in the subject through the publication of new books for the first time in very many years; this led to escalating sales of fans in European auction houses and a spate of questions from collectors for the authors and hard-pressed museum staff.

Clearly there was a need for some authoritive body which would work at a very high level through museums, art galleries, textile societies and the like. So THE FAN CIRCLE was formed with a most prestigeous selection of International Patrons at its head.

Slowly but surely the amount of members are increasing and are homing in like filings to a magnet from all parts of the world. In joining, each member increases the collective depth of knowledge on the subject, for there is nearly always some speciality that each human can eventually contribute.

Gradually the aim is to produce a world bibliography, catalogues and specialised up-to-date knowledge of museums or public collections. Equally it is hoped that a photographic library can be organised, giving evidence of the fans extant in the world and a picture built up of the fan "as art" or "as craft". No-one has undertaken such a project before but it should eventually become, with the enthusiastic help of members and friends, a composite picture of an age-old art which has never, in recent centuries, been seriously treated.

The three books were recently reviewed in FAN CIRCLE Newsletter No. 3 and they have been dealt with in chronological order:
Nancy Armstrong: A Collector's History of Fans:
Publishers: Studio Vista, London 1974. Clarkson N. Potter Inc U.S.A. 1974. Library of Congress Catalogue card 74-78079; pages 208, with black and white and colour illustrations, glossary, index and bibliography. Price $13.

A comprehensive and well-illustrated introduction to the subject from a number of collectors which treats fans thematically under technique and country of origin. There are appendices on the making of fans and on their care and collection and an up-to-date list of makers and designers.

N.B. This book is already out of print in Great Britain but good libraries should have a copy.
Bertha de Vere Green: A Collector's Guide to Fans over the Ages:
Publishers: Frederick Muller, London 1975; pages 332, with black and white and colour illustrations, index, bibliography. Price $46.

A well illustrated study of the subject, treating it chronologically. There are chapters on the cleaning and repair of fans, their assessment, the relationship of fans and decorative form; an index of makers, designs and painters and an appendix on royal owners. (Now out of print.)
Mary Gostelow: The Fan:
Publishers: Gill and Macmillan, London 1976, pages 151, black and white and colour illustrations, bibliography, index, exhibitions and useful advertisements. Price $26.

Concentrates on the fan in 16th to 20th centuries and is illustrated with a usefully diverse series of fans from a number of collections. There are sections on collections and art and the fan. There are lists of useful addresses and exhibitions.

The glue which holds together the members of THE FAN CIRCLE must be the Newsletters – questing minds need written information. To give a fair outline of the events within the CIRCLE and the way they have been presented one could do no better than quote extracts. The president, Hélène Alexander, began the first Newsletter with an explanation of how it all came about:

"On 9th April 1975, Nancy Armstrong, Martin Willcocks, Gytha Hardy and Hélène Alexander met to discuss a project which was the brain-child of R. M. Willcocks, namely that of forming a society to bring together people interested in the subject of fans. This little meeting resulted in a number of people being invited to come together on 29th April 1975 and the Fan Circle was, in fact, born. A Committee was formed, officers elected and Patrons chosen, names put forward and approved.

"After many previous months of indecision and lobbying the Fan Circle had come into being and it seemed, at the time, that all those present were delighted at the prospect of furthering the interest in a subject which was, in such a varied way, dear to them; for it was decided that the object of the Fan Circle is to promote education, i.e. source material on fans. Also to bring people together for discussions; to encourage the preservation of fine fans of all ages and from all countries and generally to benefit all those wishing to know more about fans by holding meetings and lectures, by the publication of a Newsletter and, eventually, a magazine or journal.

"A great deal of thought was accorded to 'striking the right note'. The subject of fans is one which so many lay people look upon as having a limited scope, whereas scholars, collectors and dealers all know that the possibilities of approach to the subject are endless, through the history of painting (Oriental and Western), the history of Costume, the study of the Crafts – embroidery, textiles etc etc – and so it was important that different people in different spheres should be persuaded to join the Committee. Since it was agreed that this was to be an International organisation, the choice of patrons was perhaps one of our most difficult tasks, a veritable 'Judgement of Paris' – and we all know what that poor young man got involved in!

Our Patrons

"**The Countess of Rosse** is, to fan lovers, the Princess of collectors. Hers is the famous Messel Collection which was so expertly compiled over many years by her father, the late Colonel Leonard Messel. It is a world-famous collection, for the Countess of Rosse has most generously allowed it to be written up, photographed and, indeed, a fraction shown at an Exhibition at the Victoria and Albert Museum. (In 1974 Nancy Armstrong was invited to lecture on the subject of the Messel Collection at the Victoria and Albert Museum before an audience of members of the Royal Family and four hundred of their guests from the Art World of Europe.) Now Lady Rosse has not only graciously agreed to be one of our Patrons, but has, in spite of the very busy public life she leads, given much time to take an active interest in the Fan Circle.

"**The Worshipful Company of Fan Makers** (whose Master in 1975 was Leslie Ross Collins Esq) is also represented on the Committee of the Fan Circle. Mr Ross Collins has shown, on several occasions, that the Fan Makers are an ancient Company (formed in 1708) which, very properly, while delving into the past, has its feet solidly in the 20th century.·

Mrs Doris Langley Moore, OBE, FRSL, is the distinguished author of many books and she is well known for her passionate interest in Lord Byron. We feel extremely fortunate that, in view of her involvement in the Museum of Costume and Costume Research Centre in Bath, that some of this passionate energy may some time encompass the Fan Circle.

Miss Esther Oldham is perhaps not so well known to us here in Britain, but in America hers is one of the finest collections of fans, and it is one of the best documented in the whole world. Miss Oldham has been collecting fans for a very long time and is the authority on the subject in the whole of the United States.

Like so many Americans, she has offered that inimitable hospitality to a vast number of people interested in fans and has shown a freshness of approach and enthusiasm for the project of the Fan Circle.

Photographs of her fans have appeared in many publications and it is most fortunate to think that we are so well represented overseas. (Equally it is a heart-warming thought that Miss Oldham has decided to give her collection to the Boston Museum of Fine Arts during her lifetime – to be of benefit to all.)

Mr Felix Tal is a gentleman of considerable years – though his looks belie the fact – who has been collecting fans since he was twenty years old! His vast collection touches on almost every type of fan and his visitors' book, at his home in Amsterdam, is in itself a guide to the number of people who have visited him there.

To inaugurate the Fan Circle a reception was held on Monday 3rd November 1975 in the Fan Makers' Hall, by courtesy of the Reverend Stanley Moore, Rector of St. Botolphs Without Bishopsgate, and the Master of the Worshipful Company of Fan Makers. It was a glittering affair.

The Hall itself is situated behind the church, an area where Christian worship has been offered since Roman days. The present church was designed by James Gold and consecrated in 1728, quite unique in that it is the only one of the city churches which has the tower at the East end.

The Hall behind is also the Parish Room, formerly the Ward School, built c.1860, and as you mount the steps to go in you are "greeted" by two charming figures of a boy and girl in coade stone, typical of the children who attended the school in the past.

The Worshipful Company of Fan Makers are entitled to use the Hall for their functions for twenty-four days of the year, to be agreed with the Rector. When they do so they become "en fête" with hanging banners dating back to their own Inauguration in 1708 and with glass cases round the walls displaying a lovely and historic collection of their own fans.

Fortunately three of the Fan Circle's International Patrons were able to attend the function; the Countess of Rosse came over especially from Ireland, Mrs Doris Langley Moore left her work on her latest book and the Master brought Mrs Leslie Ross Collins. Miss Esther Oldham could not come over from the United States, nor Mr Felix Tal from Holland – but everyone was sure they were with the gathering in spirit and they were often mentioned.

There were about seventy-five guests in all, including representatives of Ambassadorial Cultural Attachés and the welcoming speeches were all short, witty and to the point. As it was such a unique gathering the broadcasting press were there in full and several broadcast tapes were made for both home and overseas use…which brought a waterfall of questions by mail later on. But, in such a specialised society as the Fan Circle, it is really by word of mouth that new members are made interested enough to join".

The Fan Circle entertained in November: the Worshipful Company of Fan Makers gave their annual dinner in December and were gracious enough to invite several members of the Fan Circle as their guests – since which time Lord Rosse has been invited to become a Liveryman.

The Livery Dinner was held at the Mansion House and again I quote Mrs Hélène Alexander, the President of the Fan Circle:-

"It was a brilliant setting, for a brilliant gathering, not least of the attractions being a collection of about twelve fans lent by Her Majesty Queen Juliana of the Netherlands and brought over especially for this occasion by Mr C. A. Burgers. (The most interesting items were a pair of 'Vernis Martin' fans, one original early brisé fan with a typical Dutch genre scene – beautifully painted – while another was a nineteenth century 'pastiche' of equally high quality, but quite typically a fan of a later period, with little medallions containing family portraits, some of them children's. The centrepiece was a fine silk fan (late Victorian) with an exquisitely painted 'skyscape'.)

"The function was in the beautiful Egyptian Hall – and banquet it was indeed!

"Lady Rosse, in amethysts and diamonds, was gracious as ever. Mrs Ross Collins welcomed her guests in her own specially natural way and carried a fine white ostrich feather fan. Nancy Armstrong looked stunning in flame chiffon and she carried a red lacquer eighteenth century fan and Mrs Bertha de Vere Green was charming in cream-coloured lace and wore a beautiful fan-shaped brooch. [Hélène Alexander, herself, looked very lovely too.]

"Even in so grand a setting and with such an imposing number of dignitaries and special guests, one felt completely 'at home' especially because of the cordial welcome made to us representatives of the Fan Circle in several speeches by the Lord Mayor, Alderman Sir Lindsay Ring, the Master of the Fan Makers, the Foreign Warden (Mr N. A. Royce) and the Right Hon. Robert Carr M.P. (now Lord Carr)."

Within the first year's existence of the Fan Circle there have been three newsletters, three lectures and an exhibition mounted in the Harris Museum in Preston, Lancashire. Whatever the detractors have to say – that is an impressive record for a brand new society.

Let me quote a short report on the

Top right. *Dutch fan painted on vellum. Very fine sticks, carved and heavily painted. Sapphire-coloured rivet. c. 1760.*
Bottom right. *Very fine early brisé japanned fan showing a rustic banquet. Possibly from Spa, near Liége in Belgium. c. 1715.*
Overleaf. *18th century fan once owned by Lady Catherine Powlett, daughter of the last Duke of Bolton. Very fine painted leaf on paper, showing a biblical subject framed by a border of finely painted fruit and flowers. Mother-of-pearl sticks with "vernis-Martin-type" vignettes and mica panels.*

exhibition written up by Mrs Lisa Clinton, editor of the Fan Circle Newsletter and member of the staff at the Victoria and Albert Museum, together with Miss Avril Hart, Research Assistant in the Textile Department of the same Museum:

"The Exhibition was opened by the Right Worshipful the Mayor of Preston, and Lord Rosse addressed the distinguished gathering.

"This remarkable exhibition was organised jointly by the Fan Circle and the staff of the Harris Museum and Art Gallery and ran from 19th June to 31st July initially. Such was its success that its duration was extended until the end of September.

"The display, arranged by Mrs Hélène Alexander, President of the Fan Circle, and Mrs Alex Conway of the Harris Museum, consisted of nearly three hundred fans lent by members of the Fan Circle, Gawthorpe Hall (the Kay-Shuttleworth Trust), the Harris Museum and Art Gallery, the Merseyside County Museums, and the Victoria and Albert Museum. The fans were carefully arranged and clearly and fully labelled in top-lit cases in two large rooms, the first being devoted to late seventeenth and eighteenth century examples, and the second to those of the nineteenth and twentieth centuries, with three cases reserved for examples from the Leonard Messel Collection.

"The eighteenth century collections contained an outstanding group of 'Vernis Martin' fans, and two famous early political ones, the 'Dr Sacheverell' fan of 1710, and the Jacobite fan of 1715 lent by the Victoria and Albert Museum; a fine selection of painted fans with classical, biblical and picturesque subjects, printed fans of all types, political, puzzle, botanical and tourist; and some remarkable examples of rarer types such as the cabriolet, marriage and mourning fans. The Oriental groups included fans made for the European market as well as high quality ones – made for home consumption.

"It was particularly interesting to see such a comprehensive collection of nineteenth century fans, from early small brisé and spangled types, through fine mid-nineteenth century painted and printed ones with romantic scenes and a great variety of sticks, to the later styles using a wider range of materials and techniques.

"In addition there were three cases containing late nineteenth century and early twentieth century advertising fans and an extremely interesting case showing Indian, Indonesian and Philippino examples from 1900-1975.

"Amongst the splendid objects shown from the Messel Collection was the famous large autograph fan (which Lady Rosse graciously brought to the Inaugural Reception), fine late nineteenth century Oriental fans and the renowned 'Perdita Robinson' fan of 1775. The nineteenth century display was particularly cleverly embellished with other attractive costume accessories such as scent bottles, gloves and coloured romantic engravings supplied by the Harris Museum, and the eighteenth century room with illustrations and fan mounts lent by the Hon. Christopher Lennox Boyd.

"On the ends of the show-cases and round the walls was displayed excellent background material in the form of Japanese prints, fashion plates from English and French magazines, cartoons and illustrations from the Great Exhibition of 1851, all of which reflected the style of the fans to be seen close by and helped to place them in their fashionable context. The catalogue, with eight illustrations and thorough descriptions of all the objects, will serve as an invaluable record of the first Exhibition of the Fan Circle."

The three lectures held during the year were one on the care of fans, by Nancy Armstrong, in the Victoria and Albert Museum on 21st February 1976; a second by Santina Levey, research assistant in the Department of Textiles at the Victoria and Albert Museum on "Lace" on 6th November 1976 and a third by Avril Hart, from the same department, speaking on the museum's collection of fans on 11th December 1976. Each venue was completely different; the first in the Lecture Theatre, the second in the private home of the secretary, Mrs Gytha Hardy, and the third in the Textile Study rooms of the museum.

So, whether they are grand receptions in famous halls or intense study groups around a deliciously fattening tea-table in a private drawing room – the atmosphere is the same; exceptionally fascinated people coming together to learn, to ask questions and to give of their own knowledge as well – and taking the trouble to travel hundreds of miles to do so.

But the driving force is always written evidence, and that is contained in the Newsletters which give reports of functions and a pot-pourri of isolated items of news which make a homogenous whole.

In the first Newsletter, apart from the explanation of how the entire concept 'got off the ground' there was a chronological diary of events, details of an exhibition of the collection of Mr and Mrs John Richards of Anglesey which was put on in Llangefni Library in September 1975, and a very scholarly and erudite description of the Ickworth Collection written up by Mrs Emily Joy (her husband, the eminent furniture-historian Edward Joy, was curator there for a number of years, retiring in 1976).

Mrs Joy explained that the collection at Ickworth in Suffolk was made by the third Marchioness of Bristol between about 1870 and 1906, comprising thirty-five fans from the seventeenth to the twentieth centuries, all in very good condition as they have been so carefully looked after over the years. In fact the Marchioness of Bristol's specialised and keen interest in fans was recognised by the Worshipful Company of Fan Makers who awarded her in 1878 their Gold Medal (Class VI).

The second Newsletter gave reports on all the recent events and began to broaden out into extracts from letters and queries from other noted bodies.

One such was the Royal Institute of British Architects, which wrote to tell members that there was to be an exhibition of the work of Thomas Robins at the Heinz Gallery, 21 Portman Square in London from January until the end of March – and to ask the help of fan collectors in possibly identifying further works of this artist.

The Exhibition, called "The Gardens of Delight – the Art of Thomas Robins" included paintings and a recently discovered sketchbook by the artist, Thomas Robins of Bath (died 1770) who worked during the middle decades of the eighteenth century sketching and painting views of English houses and gardens at the height of the Rococo style. Although mainly important for its contribution to the history of English gardening in the eighteenth century, this exhibition was also of great interest to fan collectors, for Thomas Robins is known to have painted fans, and recently John Harris, Curator of the Drawings Collection at the R.I.B.A., has discovered one, showing a view of the Spa at Cheltenham and another called "Ralph Allen's Stonemason's Yard near Prior Park, Bath."

This latter is illustrated on page 69 of Nancy Armstrong's book "A Collector's History of Fans", although it was, at that time, neither associated with Thomas Robins by Nancy Armstrong nor by Christies, who sold it. According to Mr Harris and his research through the recently discovered sketchbook the new building in the background is a terrace of workmen's cottages.

This exhibition, coinciding with the formation of the Fan Circle, served as a timely reminder of the importance of looking at sources such as these for eighteenth century fan decoration.

The third Newsletter gave all the expected reports on the exhibition etc, and added various intriguing snippets such as a photograph of a canopied tombstone of a lady with a fan in the Carlisle Museum, Roman period, second to third century AD – together with the caption "Was this the first British Fan?".

There was also a report from Miss Susan Mayor of Christies, detailing a most important sale on 29th July 1976, where a most unusual French fan, c.1760, whose leaf was entirely covered with painted mother-of-pearl plaques, was sold for $1,900.

From Nancy Armstrong came (as it was Bicentennial Year) a list and description of the fans once owned by First Ladies in America, held by the Smithsonian Institution in Washington.

On 8th May 1978 the Annual General Meeting of the Fan Circle was held at the Courtauld Institute, Portman Square, London. The President of the Fan Circle gave an address which included news of the previous year's activities. She outlined the visits to Althorp, Northamptonshire in June, 1977; Waddesdon Manor, Buckinghamshire in September and the Castle Museum in York in October. There were collectors

Top right. *Advertising fan for "La Menthe Pastille", made just after the formation of the Hague International Court of Justice, showing all the nations sitting around the table; most of them drinking the advertised alcohol. c. 1910-15.*
Bottom right. *Art Deco fan in the Japanese style, painted by M. Hentiquez. c. 1925.*
Overleaf. *A fan commemorating the Peace of Amiens of 1802 between France, England, Spain and Holland. The paper leaf has a hand-coloured etching of Bonaparte and allegorical figures, and is inscribed. The ivory sticks are pierced and silvered.*

meetings in private houses such as Mr and Mrs Zarach in London in August, Mrs MacAlpine in January 1978 and Christies in May 1978. Lectures were given by Mrs Julia Hutt and Mr Joe Earle (both of the Victoria and Albert Museum) on the subject of Chinese and Japanese fans, Mr and Mrs Clegg spoke on birds' feathers and their application to fans and Nancy Armstrong was invited to give a lecture on the Oldham Collection in the Museum of Fine Arts in Boston.

One very special event was a Jubilee Reception which was held at the Hall of the Worshipful Company of Fan Makers, a reception graced by Her Royal Highness Princess Alice, who had presented the Company with many of her fans. Besides the exhibition of these and others belonging to the Company, Mrs Bertha de Vere Green

had, by special request, provided an extra display of fans, covering a vast range and variety of specimens.

The Fan Circle has now settled down and, at the same time, has opened up a huge vista for people to study. Some specialised collectors have been badly jolted by completely new avenues of thought being presented to them, whereas others have had their beliefs confirmed from diverse directions. The exciting feeling for members is that they are "in at the beginning", that they can be artistic pioneers – and that they can contribute to the crafts and/or conservation.

Certainly the exhibition "Fans from the East", being put on in Birmingham Art Gallery from 17th November 1978 – 6th January 1979 and then at the Victoria and Albert Museum from 31st January 1979 to 15th April breaks entirely new ground. The

Fan Circle are extremely grateful that these fine Museums have collaborated with them in producing an exhibition which has never, ever, been held before. In view of this Debretts Peerage are publishing a book on the subject as a whole, dealing with each of the five separate sections of the exhibition in turn; i.e. Japanese fans, Chinese fans, Chinoiserie, fans from the Seychelles to the Philippines and "A Living Art", the work of Miss Katy Talati – each section being written by the person who arranged it.

Many activities are planned far ahead; visits, collectors' meetings, lectures and conservation weekends. Everyone is welcome, whether they collect or are merely interested in the subject like myself, for I only own three fans. There could be a very bright future for the Fan Circle and its many members all over the world.

Hon. Secretary's address: 24, Asmuns Hill, London NW11 6ET.

Above. *Carved Alpine wooden fan showing small paintings of scenes of well-known villages. c. 1860.*
Left. *Small brisé Minuet or Imperceptible fan of carved and painted wood. c. 1820.*
Top right. *A fan – which has its own case – originally owned by Queen Charlotte, showing a fishing scene. Painted on kid, with carved, pierced, fretted and gilt ivory sticks.*
Bottom right. *A fan for the Spanish market depicting "Alexander saying farewell to the Family of Darius" painted on vellum. The sticks show the battoir shapes. c. 1860.*

The Repair of Fans

There is a world of interest for the fan owners prepared to mend their own damaged fans, but there is a great deal of difference between mending a fan and fan conservation.

I am not attempting, in any way, to enter into the arena of such giants in the textile conservation field as Mrs Karen Finch. Quite rightly, in a recent lecture to the Royal Society of Arts, she stressed that conservation techniques must be removable if necessary and that, in her work, there is never any attempt to fake.

When mending a fan there is often *every* attempt to fake so that the fan looks as pretty as it did before it was damaged. When auction houses sell fans they put in the quality of its condition and also "repaired" where and when it is. Some people prefer not to buy a mended fan, others prefer not to buy a broken fan and accept repairs…it is a question of choice and taste, like buyers of ivory who want it to be white – or prefer it creamy yellow.

This section, then, is on fan repairing and not on conservation. If you cannot manage the directions you could always call in an expert – yet remember how expensive a specialist's time is today and never hope for a specialist repair to be done overnight! I recommend: John Richards, Bronant, High Street, Rhosneigr, Anglesey, N. Wales.

For framing I also recommend: Mrs Janet Merrett, "Woodthorpe", South Downs Road, Hale, Cheshire.

There is such a huge amount of repair material on the market for both the amateur and the professional that the mind (and the purse) boggles at the thought. Some repair essentials have such odd-sounding names that the buyer simply cannot distinguish what each thing actually accomplishes unless they are trained scientists; as a result I intend to over-simplify my explanations to help some people without a scientific background and pray that other readers do not feel I am talking down to them.

Each of the materials, however, is tried, trusted and true as long as the directions are followed with great care. All the materials from the firm Picreator are used in the conservation departments of all the major museums, not only in Britain but all over the world. It will also become quickly obvious that directions for cleaning ivory, for instance, may just as well apply to cleaning an ivory card-case as an ivory fan – so it is hoped that these directions will benefit other forms of antique collectors as well as the fan collector.

One's attitude to mending a fan should be examined. Are you patient? Can you train yourself to leave work alone for possibly forty-eight hours before you take it up again? It's sometimes a tremendous strain to do so when you can see that the next stage is merely stitching here or glueing there and *hey presto!* your fan is ready to be admired.

Are you nimble with your fingers? Fine embroiders are splendid people to mend fans because they are trained to work evenly as well as in miniature. Have you the time? If you rush at your work you may easily do more damage than if you appear lazy; this equally applies to mending for others. There are no absolutely hard and fast rules to the repair of a fan so you must give yourself ample time for something to go wrong. Even if you have cleaned and mended twenty small ivory minuet fans and found they took three days each – on the twenty-first occasion you might find that the rivet won't unscrew for you to clean between the sticks at the base and the fan takes a week to deal with in the end.

Have you the opportunity of having a small room for your own work? If you have no intention at all of mending more than one or two fans this would be unnecessary, but it is curious how infectious fan-mending can become; once you are known to mend your fans it will become inevitable that a friend will ask you to do their's – or a parasol – or the good binding of a Georgian book – or a mother-of-pearl tea-caddy and, before you know what has happened you are in business.

Do you need the money? Because if you need money you would be better advised to take an ordinary job doing something else. Once you reckon up your time and labour you might easily feel resentful that you are not earning a fortune for your patience and expertise – but there is a very big difference between mending fans as a career, as a job or as a hobby. To make it a career you would need a great deal of capital to tide you over for about five years; to mend fans as a job would mean that you would lose money hand-over-fist in comparison to doing other jobs at x amount per hour.

The only way to look at it is to mend fans as a hobby, getting nothing out of it except for pure happy satisfaction that you have made something lovely out of something torn or broken. Should you decide to mend fans in your own small private room, which you could lock, then I would suggest that the following materials would be necessary – many would be available in your own home anyway:

General materials for mending fans in your workshop.

A large flannelette sheet, preferably white.
Plastic bags.
Pieces of fine split cane.
Large angled magnifying glass (leaving the hands free) the bigger the better. I suggest you write to John Dudley & Co, Ltd Dept DT82, 301 Cricklewood Lane, Finchley Rd, London N.W.2. for a Fine Work Magnifier.
Sloping stand, like a book stand for a table. I had mine made of white plastic-type material with two small adjustable legs at the back which raise or lower the height of the stand. It has a small ledge at the front, about two inches deep, so the rivets of the fans would rest on the ledge, and is altogether twenty-two inches wide and sixteen inches high. I use this to work on the fan some of the time, it saves a violent crick in the neck at having to work with your head bent over the fan lying on a table quite flat.

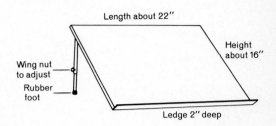

Work stand

A bobbin drill for making holes in ivory, pearl etc.
Small pair of pincers.
Set of needle files.
Six-way leather punch.
Cosmetics brushes.
Baby's tooth brushes.
Cotton wool.
Tissue paper of the best quality only. White is best with a final sheet of black wrapped around the white at the end to try and keep out the light when wrapping a fan. Don't use black directly onto a fan *just in case* the dye comes off in faintly damp conditions.
Wooden cocktail sticks.
Wooden clothes pegs – never plastic because they stick to modern adhesives and are impossible to remove without damaging all your work.
Several small palettes or odd saucers for paint or adhesives. These will never go back again into your pantry, so don't use anything you want to keep; however good your intentions, one day the phone will ring when you are mixing an everlasting adhesive on your best Coalport and that will be that. It's as easy to use flat dishes as saucer types for you only ever use a minute amount of adhesive or paint at a time. Always use china or glass, never plastic.
Nail file.
Emery boards or emery paper.
Rasp.
Selection of coloured ribbons for nineteenth century loops at the rivet. It is wise to wait until you have the fan to re-ribbon before you buy these, but once you have them do buy an extra amount – many fans have the same colourings and you can save time and expense by stocking up on various shades of pink which seem indigenous to the Victorian era etc. The ribbons should be a quarter of an inch to one inch wide, of pastel shades and preferably made from silk.
Very fine sewing needles and Milwards Beading needles. These can bend and distort after a while from the heat of your hand so it is best if you warm the distorted needle and put it back, straight, in its case or against a flat surface. It is best to change the needles continually as you work *before* they distort.

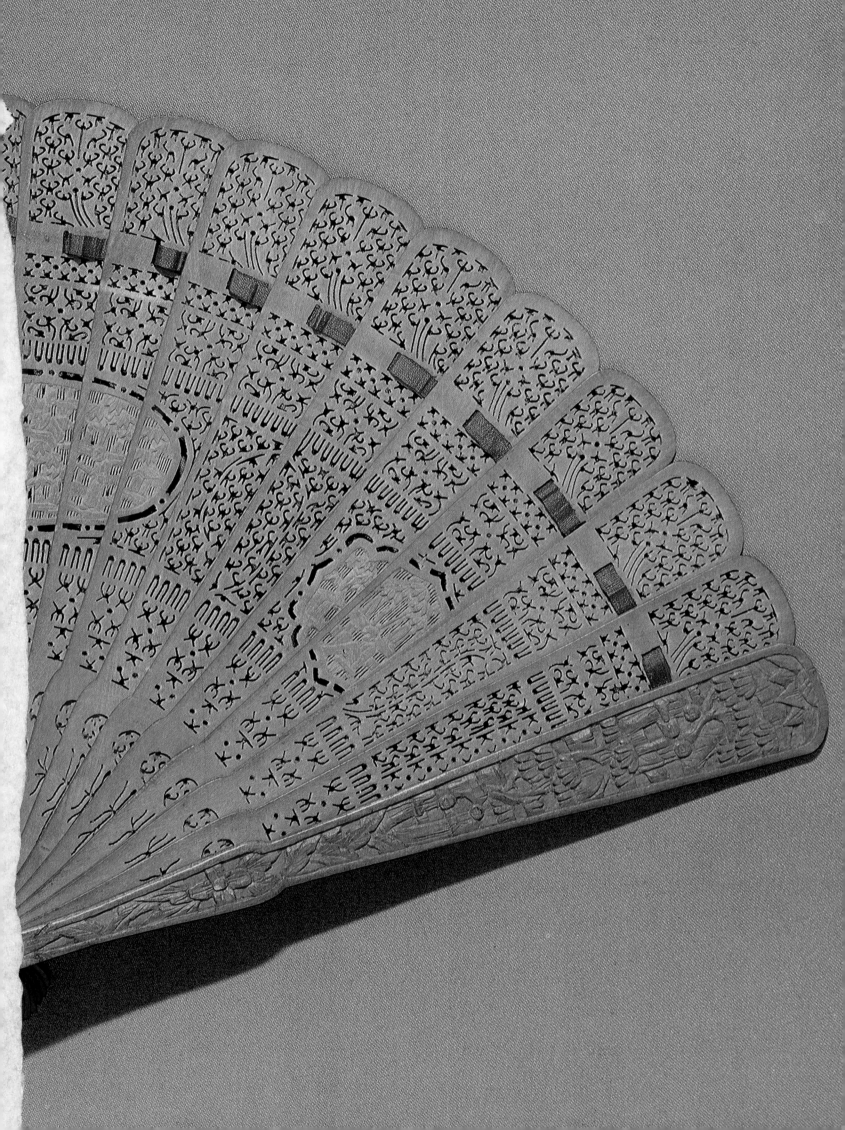

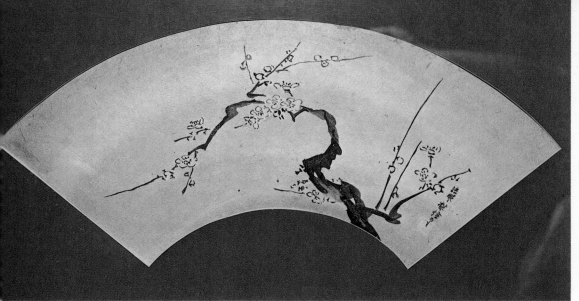

parts of weight in one hundred parts of volume. Stir in quickly until dissolved; if you remove the mixture from the source of heat it may gel or thicken slightly but reheating restores the solution. It is best to keep the mixture at the correct temperature during the working session. Apply the mixture by spray-blowing it over torn fabric or chicken-skin, or just paint it on if the material is fairly firm. Either use a small polythene spray-bottle or a spray-diffuser (from an art shop) and then leave the material to dry.

Use very small amounts at a time as the spirit quickly evaporates. It is important to clean your spray with clean warm solvent, for the mixture would otherwise block the orifice.

There are no visible after-effects but there is inevitably a fractional amount of stiffening. This might mean the rivet of a fan should be slightly loosened to avoid the risk of distortion when the leaf is covered with Calaton and then re-pleated – but it is not always necessary.

Cellofas. Supplied by Picreator Enterprises Ltd, 44 Park View Gardens, London NW4 2PN. In America the suppliers are either Talas, 104 Fifth Avenue, New York, New York 10011 or you can get it at Alfa Products, Ventron Corporation, 152 Andover Street, Danvers, Mass. 01923.

This is a water soluble adhesive in granules and looks and behaves like a very refined wall-paper paste. When using it mix a very small amount of granules with warm water – use bottled or distilled water – and thoroughly stir for some time. It thickens up considerably and one must gauge with time how thick it should be for use. Nets or laces need it thinner, heavy papers can do with it thicker. It is invaluable to hold Nylon Net or Nylon Gossamer Fabric on torn textiles, vellum or paper.

Dried-up paste remaining in the mixing-pot can soon be regenerated by adding a little warm water. Since this material is an attractive food for some bacteria or insects, it is advisable to add a small amount of Dowicide A before use. Make up a ten percent solution of Dowicide in water and add just a few drops to the Cellofas solution. Dowicide is potent in concentration as low as ten parts per million.

Dowicide A. Only available from Picreator Enterprises Ltd., 44 Park View Gardens, London NW4 2PN. This is a water-soluble fungicide/bactericide and something fan collectors should consider very carefully… too few collectors are aware of the insects which invade their fans, especially those with feathers involved. No fan should be considered cleaned and repaired until they have had some form of fungicide/bactericide applied. There is a choice, see also Mystox.

Vulpex Liquid Soap. Supplied only by Picreator Enterprises Ltd., 44 Park View

Large and small paint brushes of the best quality you can afford.

Tiny needlework scissors, which must be kept sharpened.

Eyebrow tweezers with flat ends; these must be cleaned regularly with adhesive solvents otherwise they will become useless from clogging.

Jewellery long-nosed pliers.

Razor blades, which are dangerous to materials unless used with the greatest of care.

Short lengths of wire from your iron-mongers for ostrich feather spines; they must be stiff enough to hold but not too stiff that you cannot bend them at one end with a small pair of pliers. Thin wire coat-hangers from dry-cleaners can be used; they are rigid and rustproofed.

Tape measure.

Labels. The best ones are white, with cotton tags, from your local stationers, about one to one and a half inches long.

Strips of wood.

Reels of thread, preferably silk, of various pastel colours and black and white.

Non-rusting pins.

Surgical spirit from a chemist.

Pastry board.

Distilled water in a small air-tight container.

Pieces of clean linen or cotton about twice the size of your fan.

Brown paper for packing fans.

Corrugated cardboard.

Large boxes, tennis-ball containers or moulded wine-bottle containers.

String.

Large pair of scissors.

Gumstrip and/or sticky tapes. The only time you ever use pressure sensitive adhesive tapes is on the outside of a parcel, NEVER on a fan.

Specialised materials for repairing fans.

Please send a SAE (at least nine inches by four) to manufacturers when requesting literature – overseas visitors should also send an International Reply Coupon.

Calaton. Supplied by Picreator Enterprises Ltd., 44 Park View Gardens, London NW4 2PN. In America the suppliers are either Talas, 104 Fifth Avenue, New York, N.Y. 10011 or you can get it at Alfa Products, Ventron Corporation, 152 Andover Street, Danvers, Mass. 01923.

This is a soluble nylon powder, an adhesive for fragile and extremely delicate objects and forms a very fine, matt and virtually undetectable film, holding fragments firmly together. The film, which remains slightly porous to atmospheric moisture, does not exert surface tension so will not distort the leaf.

When using, warm a little surgical spirit in a small bowl in a saucepan of very hot water. PAY PARTICULAR ATTENTION TO FIRE RISKS. Then add two percent of Calaton crystals; in other words two grams in one hundred millilitres of surgical spirits or two

Top. *Japanese folding fan – "Plum Blossom" – painted by Kano Tanshin (1653-1718). Ink on paper with gold wash. Signed: Hogen Tanshin hitsu, and with a seal.*

Left. *Chinese folding fan, embroidered in the 18th century with birds and flowers.*

Gardens, London NW4 2PN. It is potassium methyl cyclohexyl oleate, used for cleaning textiles, ivory or leather. For textiles, such as lace, you find it is soluble in water (two to five percent) and for cleaning ivory or leather use it with white spirit.

Mystox LPL. Supplied only by Picreator Enterprises Ltd., 44 Park View Gardens, London NW4 2PN, or Alfa Products, Ventron Corporation, 152 Andover Street, Danvers, Mass. 01923. This is an essential protective for looking after fans. Technically it is pentachlorophenyl laurate, one hundred percent concentrate; a fungicide/bactericide/insecticide for all natural fibres, textiles, leather, wood etc. Treated materials are perfectly safe to handle as Mystox proves no hazard to higher animal life: it is lethal ONLY to insects, bacteria etc…but, even so, use it with plenty of fresh air around at the time. Use five percent Mystox LPL in white spirit or surgical spirit and paint or spray on. It gives at least ten years' protection and is a permanent moth-proofer.

Filtration Fabric. Supplied only by Picreator Enterprises Ltd., 44 Park View Gardens, London NW4 2PN. An open-grid fabric of heavy-duty glass-grade PVC for overlay and vacuum-cleaning of fans. (It looks like a white or cream miniature tennis-net and it is stiff.) It can be used again and again; it can also be used as a support for lace-washing.

Nylon Net. Supplied only by Picreator Enterprises Ltd., 44 Park View Gardens, London NW4 2PN. This net and the following Nylon Gossamer Fabric are the most important parts of fan repairing. It is an extruded net with a regular mesh, 20 denier, ivory coloured, non-fraying and used to consolidate frayed textiles.

Nylon Gossamer Fabric. Supplied only by Picreator Enterprises Ltd., 44 Park View Gardens, London NW4 2PN. I found that this was my most valuable asset when mending fans. It is an ultra-fine transparent non-woven nylon fabric, for bonding textiles, chicken-skin, paper etc, using an adhesive such as Cellofas or Calaton. It has no grain and therefore fits into every background like the finest spider's web and can scarcely be seen afterwards. It can take dyes and you can also print and paint on it.

Renaissance Wax Polish. Manufactured by Picreator Enterprises Ltd., 44 Park View Gardens, London NW4 2PN; in America the two suppliers are either Talas, 104 Fifth Avenue, New York, New York 10011., or Alfa Products, Ventron Corporation, 152 Andover Street, Danvers, Mass. 01923. It is invaluable for anything which needs a protective polish – fans, furniture or books. It is a micro-crystalline wax cleaner and polisher,

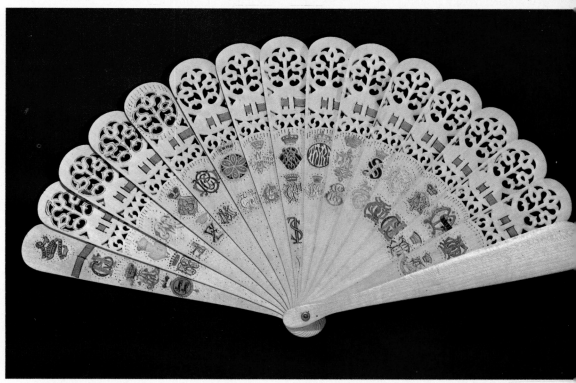

Top right. *An early English fan, c. 1720, with a painted design on vellum. The ivory sticks are overlapping and have delicate silk piqué, the guards clouté with mother-of-pearl and piqué.*

Centre right. *Wooden brisé fan with cut-out crests pasted onto the wood to make the design. Viennese. c. 1880.*

Bottom right. *An advertising fan showing a lady piloting an aeroplane. c. 1910. This fan advertises Piver's perfumes on the reverse; some are even overprinted with "Carlo Maestrani's Grand Café Central Restaurant, Folkestone.*

imparting a glass-clear coating of wax which will not stain surfaces in the course of time or through exposure to light, nor damage or alter any original decorated surfaces. It is invaluable.

Limousine Wax Polish. Manufactured and supplied by Picreator Enterprises Ltd., 44 Park View Gardens, London NW4 2PN and in America only by Talas, 104 Fifth Avenue, New York, New York 10011. This is another micro-crystalline wax cleaner and polisher with an identical blend of waxes as in Renaissance Wax Polish but incorporating special inhibitors of metal corrosion and leather mould.

Pre-lim Surface Cleaner. Manufactured and supplied by Picreator Enterprises Ltd., 44 Park View Gardens, London NW4 2PN and in America only by Talas, 104 Fifth Avenue, New York, New York 10011. A mildly-abrasive cream for safely removing oxidised grime and stains from all surfaces, especially polished wood and ivory. It leaves no marks and when polished imparts a slight surface shine.

Groom/stick. Manufactured and supplied by Picreator Enterprises Ltd., 44 Park View Gardens, London NW4 2PN. This is a completely new type of cleaner, basically made of a type of rubber which always remains tacky. It is a molecular trap, a unique long-life absorptive cleaner for many surfaces. To use: cut or tear off a small piece, shape into a cigar and roll it across a dirty surface, lightly. Stretch/twist/fold the rubber a few times to regain its tackiness and use again and again until it has absorbed several times its own weight of surface dirt. This is especially good for cleaning dirt trapped in ornamentally carved surfaces – (where a DRY cleaner is preferred to wet, such as ivory) – just press Groom/stick into the surface and peel back the rubber. No matter how dirty it becomes it always handles cleanly. Groom/stick is ideal for cleaning paper fan-leaves and all types of carved fan-sticks and guards. Sold in 100g packs.

Morden Fluorescent Tube Jackets. Supplied by The Morden Company, Harding Street, Exchange, Salford M3 7AH. Fluorescent lighting tubes cause fading because of the ultra-violet emanations from the lighting. This can damage fans kept in special cases, giving both discoloration of dyes and deterioration of textiles. The Morden tube jackets absorb about ninety-eight percent of the ultra-violet rays, are long lasting and can be cut from their normal length of forty-eight inches long (1220 mm) and one and a half inches diameter (38 mm) to the length required.

Silica Gel. Supplied by Picreator Enterprises Ltd., 44 Park View Gardens, London NW4 2PN in fifty or one hundred gram packs; it is also available in a variety of other places. Silica gel (a special self-indicating type) is a crystalline substance which absorbs atmospheric moisture in a closed container, changing colour from blue to pink as it reaches its saturation point. Warming the material in a cool oven drives off the moisture and restores the original blue tint. The substance is re-usable at least six times, after which it should be replaced.

Alec Tiranti Ltd., 21 Goodge Place, London W1. This firm is internationally known as suppliers of all tools and materials for sculptors, woodworkers and artists. They have a large range of books on all forms of the arts, especially the practical, and can supply a catalogue.

Allan's of Duke Street Ltd., 56 Duke Street, London W1M 6HS for possible supplies of new lace, fine silks and tafettas. They are a very high quality shop and if anyone in the country has a rarity it would be found at Allan's.

F. Friedlein & Co. Ltd., 718/720 Old Ford Road, London E3 2TA for both ivory and tortoiseshell, large areas or offcuts; buy as much as you can because of the growing shortages. But do not hesitate to go there personally – ivory and tortoiseshell varies greatly in colour and texture and you should take a matching piece with you in order to check. It is best to go by car if you can, otherwise leave half a day from the centre of London to get there, find the place, choose your materials and return. You will receive a great deal of help and advice.

Charles Singleton Ltd., Church Lane, Hackenthorpe, Sheffield S12 4AN for mother-of-pearl in any form – white, some colours and abalone shell. You should write and ask for "blanks", stating the length you require: i.e. a bar three inches long by half an inch wide and five-eighths thick is about standard. They also provide mother-of-pearl sequins; these are very sensible to use when a lace fan has had its sequins rust upon the fabric. You can remove the rusted sequin and replace with a mother-of-pearl one (and invisible thread) which does not glare out at you as much as a new gold or silver sequin would do.

Imperial Chemical Industries Ltd., Organic Division, P.O. Box 42, Blakeley, Manchester M9 3DA, for advice over dyeing mother-of-pearl, or write to Picreator Enterprises Ltd. This is a highly specialised task and should be treated with great caution. It's almost better to use similar mother-of-pearl from another fan but if this is simply not possible write to I.C.I.

Paperchase, 216 Tottenham Court Road, London W1 for all supplies of paper – European and Oriental; gold and silver foils etc.

Blutack. A blob of Blutack fastens or holds cleanly. Available in stationers.

Joy cellulose thinner. Available in Art shops etc.

Kleintex invisible threads. Available in most general stores.

Gilding materials: There is quite a variety and the most effective way is to use several different types at the same time, giving a "quatre couleur" effect, which does not look brand new: Goldfinger, Run 'n Buff, Renaissance Liquid Leaf, Kandahar Silver, Liquid Gold Leaf, Liquid Silver Leaf. Available, with advice, from most good Art shops.

Humbrol Multicraft No. 5. Kit of scalpels, knives and gouges.

Windsor and Newton's Designer's Gouache Paints, introductory set of ten.

Blotting paper.

Polyclens Plus for cleaning brushes properly.

Silvo.

Dissolvex for removing Araldite and some other impact adhesives.

Acetone will dissolve some glues.

Adhesives: these must always be used exactly as the directions state, for very few are reversible on a fan.

Durofix. This is a celluloid cement, and it is extremely useful as it is transparent, so that it can be built up in layers to form a self-supporting film. One great advantage of Durofix is that it is a "one-tube" adhesive and does not have to be mixed with a hardener.

Evostik is a reliable contact adhesive and made in several types; however in all cases the parts to be joined are brought directly together on impact – so complete accuracy is essential.

Cascamite. This is a powder glue which is mixed with water and good for use with woods, especially the soft fruit woods often used for fan sticks.

Aerolite. This a powder mixed with a liquid hardener, making a very strong resin adhesive.

Pastes. Special pastes such as Gripfix and photographic mounting pastes are most useful for paper work as they do not cause cockling or staining.

Copydex. This is an extremely useful white, opaque, rubber-based adhesive for all fabrics and textiles.

Araldite. The great stand-by for fan repairers. It is excellent in the two-tube pack (A.V.100 and H.V.100). All objects should be first cleaned, de-greased and dried. Mix the Araldite on a small piece of glass. Keep some methylated sprits handy for cleaning up, as it will dissolve Araldite while it is still soft. It is important that the contents of the tubes never mix except as and when you want them. When using them, warm the two tubes before measuring out and mixing; it makes it thinner, easier to use, but takes a little longer to set. It takes twelve hours to set at room temperature and three days to harden to maximum strength. The Rapid type takes less time, but it is worth leaving for absolute certainty.

Calaton. Mentioned above.

Cellofas. Mentioned above.

Bleaching Ivory. To make up a bleaching paste mix Whiting and 20 volume hydrogen peroxide into a stiff paste. The paste MUST be stiff or the ivory will absorb too much liquid, swell and distort. Coat the ivory with the paste, stand it out in the air and sunshine until the paste has dried, then wash it off and dry the piece thoroughly with a soft clean cloth. A little almond oil applied with a soft rag will leave a good protective coating, or

Top right. *Victorian fan, c. 1860, with an 18th century pastiche scene painted in the central vignette. Mother-of-pearl sticks and guards. Silvered and gilded.*

Bottom right. *Victorian fan. c. 1860. Lithographed leaf with a family scene. The ivory sticks are pierced and worked with a chequerboard silvered motif.*

Overleaf. *A fan of 1899 with a chicken-skin leaf painted with nasturtiums and signed 'Emma Fanty Lescure'. The guards applied with pierced gold panels enamelled in subtle pinks, yellow and green lilies, daisies and roses in the Art Nouveau style, with enamelled gold handle by Paul Telfe of Berlin, and a flower pivot.*

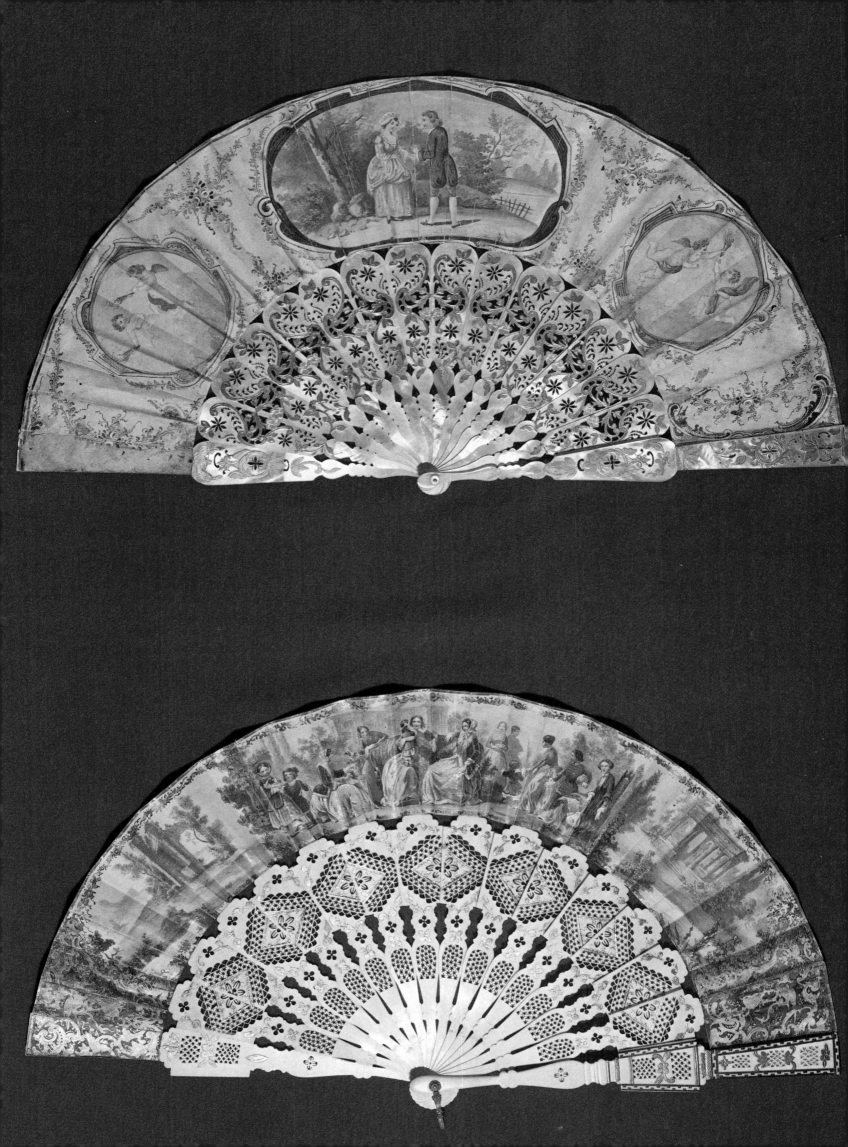

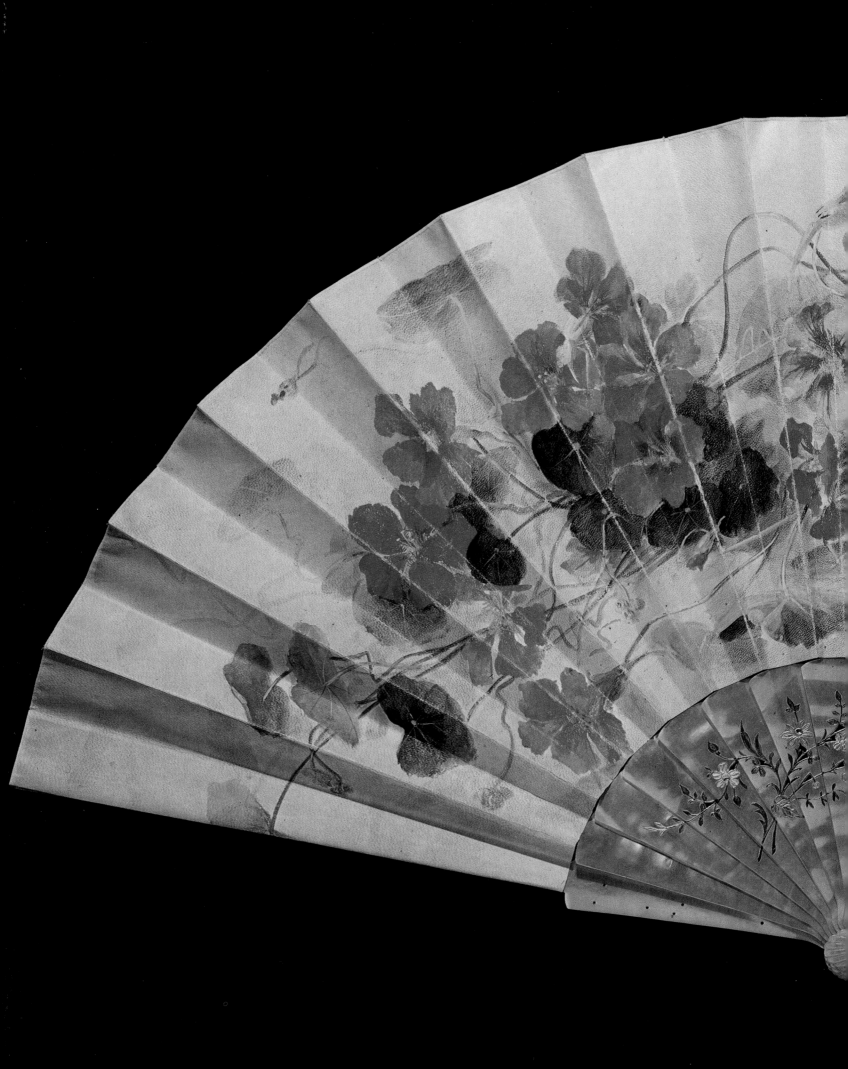

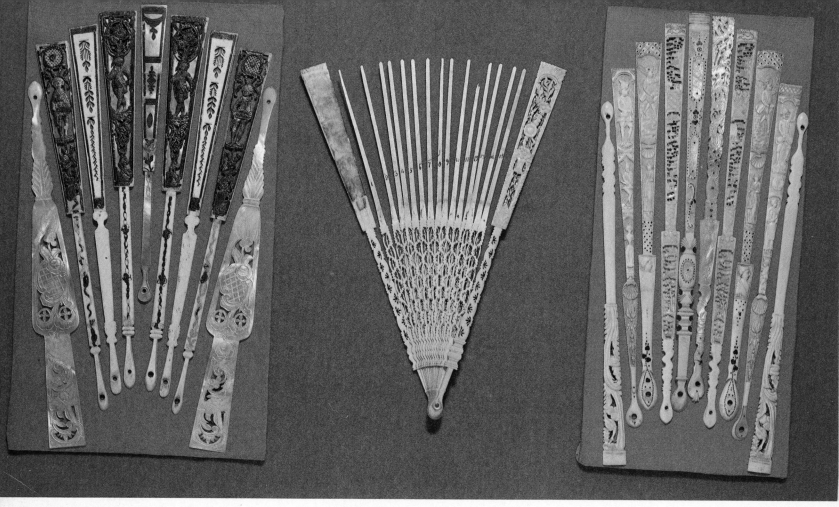

use Renaissance polish, *but not both together.*

Cleaning Ivory or Bone. Never use water, it swells the ivory or bone and then you have distorting and straining on parts such as the rivet. Use Pre-lim; very dirty small spots can be treated with whiting and methylated spirits. Finish off with Renaissance polish.

The Work Room. Having assembled the materials you might need you will then have to prepare your room for work. It must be comfortable and warm. If you find you work best with some form of light music on all the time then make sure it is available. Otherwise make sure that you can work in utter peace and quiet by taking the phone off the hook for the time you have allocated yourself.

On no account must you be disturbed in any way, especially when you are in the middle of applying an impact adhesive.

Working on fans is tense work, done in miniature and with total concentration. Unless you are used to this you should set aside a certain period in which to work, otherwise your neck and shoulders will ache with the nervous strain. I suggest two hour stretches are about right. Then I stand on my head for ten minutes to get the circulation going round again – but that is not everyone's choice. Perhaps a quick walk in the garden? Or a cup of tea and a glance at a book? Anything to lessen the tension of concentration.

You will need some form of table space which will not spoil; I find that a trestle table is ideal because there is plenty of room for you to cross your legs underneath…but any table which makes you feel comfortable is right.

Cover this table with a flannelette sheet which has been doubled. Fragile fans need to rest upon a soft surface and the flannelette is

ideal for this. It is also very good at absorbing any liquids which have spilt very quickly; I once saw dirty paint-water spill across a semi-polished table and sweep into a fragile silk fan, absolutely ruining it…if there had been the sheet it would not have travelled more than an inch. Equally the fabric cushions any ivory or tortoiseshell which might be fractured and tiny sequins and spangles don't skid off the fabric but stay where they are.

It is advisable to turn your sheet every day, at the end of your work period, so that any small objects can be rescued and put away, (eyebrow tweezers, a fine needle) rather than become missing when needed. At the same time you can see if the sheet needs washing, which should be done often, because cleanliness is essential.

Lighting is all-important. It is best to sit with the light slightly to one side of your body when working; not coming from behind as you would then shield it from yourself, not coming from dead ahead as the fan shields it from your view. I prefer the main daylight to come from my right side, as I am right-handed, and I like to sit near the window.

One must always, however, have some form of direct light under which to work and which can be moved around to suit yourself; a table lamp which can be re-arranged at various angles is perfect, but it must have a very heavy base so that it will never knock over and smash your fans.

Light can damage. Once you have finished working on a fan you should always shield it from the light from then onwards. So, until your fan is ready to put back into its case, box or drawer, cover it with some light greaseproof paper, covered with a sheet of black tissue paper. It is better, when fans are spread out to dry off, NOT to use clean linen

or cotton *just in case* this fabric snags an edge somewhere that you may have forgotten when you come to work the next day. Greaseproof paper allows the air to circulate, does not trap damp and will not stick to anything important. But remember to keep the black tissue paper outside *just in case* the faintest trace of damp might absorb the colour onto the fan.

Wear a short-sleeved garment. It is quite amazing how many tiny things can catch into the woollen cuff of a cardigan. The ideal garment is a cotton overall with short sleeves and a generous skirt overlay which would catch anything that falls. Endless small things fall – some of them just blow away with a breath – and they must fall softly and stay where they are. An errant but rare silver spangle would fall onto the cotton material of your lap and stay put, whereas if you were wearing nylon the spangle would slide off onto the floor and into oblivion.

On the other hand, if you are generously endowed with nylon overalls you could lay a small hand towel across your lap whilst working, as long as you remember you are doing so – on getting up you could spill everything onto the floor if you did not.

Top. *Two panels – normally framed – which show a variety of guardsticks, carved and pierced, of ivory and mother-of-pearl. In the centre is shown a set of fine 18th century ivory sticks awaiting a leaf; each stick with a number pencilled onto it.*
Top right. *Horn brisé fan, very fine quality with lacy motif and gilding. c. 1820.*
Bottom right. *Dutch or North German fan with a finely-painted rural scene on paper. The sticks are of mother-of-pearl, magnificently carved with small insects, animals and birds in the ovals, with alternate sticks silvered and gilded. Paste rivet. c. 1820.*

Place your fan on your sloping stand and examine it with a strong magnifying glass. If you are mending someone else's fan I suggest you should take the following precautions:-

1. Have two people there when the fan is unwrapped from its parcel.

2. Photograph the parcel if its condition appears disastrous or you can feel things are adrift inside – it is worst when it rattles.

3. Photograph the fan, both sides, in colour, with an instant camera.

4. Attach your own label to it, giving it a reference number.

5. Measure it for the sake of reference.

6. Write a full description of the fan. Then write a full description of the damage. Get your observer to initial this as well.

7. Send a copy of the details to the owner together with an estimate for the work involved. You will have to estimate how many hours it is going to take to mend and how much the materials will cost. Always take care to say that you cannot give a guaranteed time limit as to its return. Then send it Recorded Delivery to the owner and wait for the estimate to be accepted IN WRITING before you begin work on it – a phone-call is definitely NOT good enough.

Now you are ready to go ahead with your work. Here are some simple rules:

1. Always work from the centre outwards on a fan; tension is vital.

2. Always work from the rivet to the edge.

3. Always cover the work at night and lightly secure.

4. Always close the door of your workroom so that no child or animal enters.

5. Always throw away all liquids, paints, pastes every day.

6. Always clean all your tools and paintbrushes every day.

7. Always wash your hands AT LEAST once an hour, whatever you are doing.

8. Never rush your work: probably the fan has been around for over one hundred years

Parts of a fan

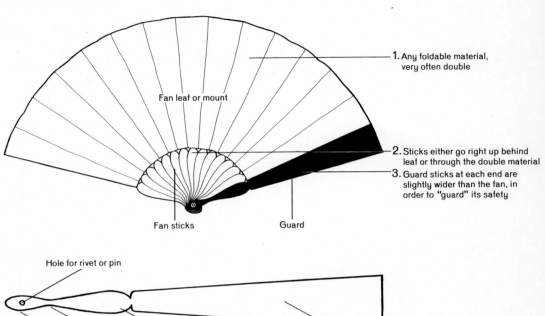

Fan leaf or mount

1. Any foldable material, very often double

2. Sticks either go right up behind leaf or through the double material

3. Guard sticks at each end are slightly wider than the fan, in order to "guard" its safety

Fan sticks

Guard

Hole for rivet or pin

Head   Gorge   Shoulder

Guard proper

or more and another day or two won't hurt. Cleanliness and method must be your aim and working in miniature your aptitude.

Mending Fan Sticks

Before you begin to mend any of your fans it is wise to treat your collection in as professional a manner as possible. Even if you have merely five fans they are still an asset in terms of beauty, money and insurance and it would repay you to deal with them as follows:

1. Examine your fan minutely under a magnifying glass, both sides.

2. Measure your fan in terms of inches and centimetres; now that we are members of the Common Market, fans for sale are measured thus. So measure the length of the guards, the length of the sticks, the width of the leaf and the total spread. That is, if the fan is quite "normal". Many fans have curious characteristics and there are no hard and fast rules about the measurements of, say, a Japanese fixed fan other than sheer common sense. Overdo it rather than leave out relevant details.

3. Photograph your fan, both back and front, three times each (six photos) in colour, with an instant camera. This way there are no negatives which can be used by unscrupulous people. See that the colour on the photograph is accurate for memory is not to be relied upon.

4. Give the fan your own personal catalogue number. Add this number to the reverse of the photographs of that fan.

5. Describe your fan with every possible detail and make three copies of your description. Give details in whichever order seems appropriate to you of: (a) The material of the sticks: whether they are ivory,

wood, tortoiseshell etc. (b) Describe every extra detail on the sticks. (c) Describe every extra detail on the guards, for they are rarely exactly the same as the sticks. (d) Describe the material of the rivet: whether it screws in or is riveted into place and if there is a button as well. (e) Describe the material the leaf is made from and whether it is a double leaf (stuck together) or a single leaf. (f)

Left. *Irregular shaped fan made of parakeet feathers and maribou, decorated with a tiny, stuffed humming-bird with a scarlet head, and a tremblant spray of flowers and leaves, all made from feathers. Together with this come two wreathes for the head, of flowers, buds and leaves – also made from feathers. Made by Melles M & E Natté, Rio de Janeiro, Brazil. c. 1850.*

Top right. *Very large Art Nouveau fan of double gold net, embroidered as a peacock with tinsel threads, silver sequins and spangles and green paste. Sticks of blonde tortoiseshell. c. 1890. English or French.*

Right. *Cockade fan of English greenhorn with cut-steels piqué-work and a quizzing-glass set in the central pivot. c. 1810-20!*

Overleaf. *French Louis XV fan with a well-painted leaf and fine sticks of mother-of-pearl, gilt and silvered, with some backing of goldfish mother-of-pearl.*

Describe the composition on the obverse side, together with the colouring and any lettering or signatures or publisher's dates. (g) Do the same for the reverse side. (h) Describe any further additions on the leaf such as sequins, spangles, straw-work, feathers, gimp, gold wires, gold edging etc. (i) Give details as to when it was acquired. (j) From whom? (k) How much it cost if it was bought; if it was bought at an auction sale it would be wise to keep the catalogue entry. (l) If it has been repaired at any time and by whom. (m) Any further documentation to prove its history.

6. Make three copies of the measurements and descriptions. Then take three large envelopes and put one copy into each envelope and add a photograph of the back and the front into each as well. Put one set in your own bank for insurance purposes. Keep one set in your own home, in a safe place and certainly NOT in the fan case or fan workroom in case of theft, for your own personal reference. Send a third to the Fan Circle, HOWEVER MODEST, to be kept in the archives which the public cannot see; this will both assist with future fan historians and the Fraud Squad in cases of theft.

Of course this is not mandatory, but anyone interested enough to read this book will have, I hope, a certain sympathy towards the aims of the Fan Circle and a spreading of knowledge about fans from a very high level – and it would be enormously helpful towards general research.

By cataloguing fans in this way a great service is done for all collectors and, gradually, it is hoped that most remaining fans will be documented. Already Mrs Hélène Alexander has catalogued the seven hundred or more fans in the York Castle Museum Collection and a great deal of interest has come to light.

7. If the fan is not housed in its own shaped box, nor its glazed case upon the wall, then it is best to place it in a piece of clean white cotton or linen material – old pillow-cases are splendid. Do not place a rubber band around any part of the fan because it can be too tight and the fan would slowly begin to distort and/or the rivet would weaken and come apart. On the other hand you can put a rubber band on the outside of the linen, very gently, just to hold it all in place.

8. Never place a fan in a plastic bag for storage; atmospheric conditions alter and somehow damp tends to become trapped inside. It is better to keep the fan in the linen or cotton wrapping with a small bag of Silica Gell alongside it, so that damp is immediately recognisable.

9. Ideally the fan in its wrappings is then covered with a sheet of black tissue paper and laid in a shallow drawer, with nothing on top. Try to avoid using velvet for the drawer as anything "walks" on the surface of velvet and, when the drawer is opened, the fan might easily bang against the wooden sides and damage. Some people have been known to use a thin sheet of polystyrene foam to bed fans down – but there is a serious fire risk in doing this as the polystyrene would burn and melt. It is better to use something matt and soft for the bottom layer of the drawer. Then place on it the fan in its wrappings, adjacent to the bag of Silica Gel (you can easily make a form of "Dorothy bag" of Nylon Gossamer Fabric in two minutes) and then edge the drawer with a strip of velvet. Paint the velvet with a 10% solution of Mystox in white spirit and, just to be safe, paint all the interior drawer surfaces, allowing to dry well before use. This precaution should effectively proof the drawer and its contents for many years against insects, bacteria and fungus growth.

10. Label the fan outside, as well as inside, with the catalogue number only. This will save you from opening it up again and again, as you should have the catalogue details available, rescuing it from wear and tear.

In General

1. Do not use water on your fan as it can affect textiles, ivory and wood in various ways. If water *has* to be used, make sure it is distilled water.

2. Always work AWAY from your own body on a fan; this somehow makes you take a great deal more care as it is a slightly unnatural function. In a curious way, when you work towards your own body, it can become over-easy, you become too confident, the hand slips and disaster comes in a twinkling.

3. Always use only minute amounts at a time of various preparations in flat, shallow dishes; liquids can ruin a fan if accidentally spilled.

4. Only deal with one side of your fan leaf or sticks each day. Allow it to rest, to breathe, and often on the next day you see something with your rested eyes you have missed. Very close work in miniature is most tiring and then one becomes careless; stop the moment you feel tired…it's always worth doing so and preventing accidents.

5. No fan should be mended without first being cleaned as well. Once cleaned the problems of mending could become both clearer and easier and, once this is done, the fan should be protected for the future against moths, fungus, bacteria and so on. So, where possible, Mystox LPL solution should be applied on both leaf and sticks, followed by Renaissance polish to non-textile surfaces (wood, paper, ivory, vellum etc).

6. When working with a damaged fan: (a) Always deal with the sticks and guards first for they are the backbone and strength of your fan. If they are not perfect then your fan leaf will sit awkwardly. Then cope with the leaf. (b) If two sticks and a guard are broken then you must deal with the guard first and the sticks afterwards. If a guard is mended badly the whole fan will be wrong; it is also the most visible part of the fan, as well as being the strongest, so it must be perfect.

Removing old adhesives

Sometimes, in the past, owners used stamp hinges to hold things together, whether the leaf or the sticks. More recently they have used pressure sensitive adhesive tapes… which is normally a benefit, but on fans is quite disastrous. Patience is needed to remove any form of adhesive at all. Some glues are removed by Dissolvex or Acetone, you will just have to experiment; otherwise, for stamp hinges I would suggest:

1. Damp a cotton-wool swab on a wooden cocktail stick with ordinary warm distilled water. Only use a drop or two, it must not be soaking wet, just damp.

2. Touch the outer surface of the stamp hinge with your swab. It soaks in quickly and it is best to deal with about four or five hinges at a time. Give them a moment to settle down.

3. Attempt to lift off the hinges with your eyebrow tweezers very carefully. Never try to lift hinges etc when dry; you will remove everything within sight if you do. If it is proving difficult you will have to wait a while, put on a drop or two more of distilled water and try again.

4. Remove the gum left behind with either a touch of dilute household ammonia on a swab, or Evostik cleaner on a swab, or cellulose thinner on a swab or white spirit on a swab – you have to experiment. Some Victorian stamp hinges were made from a water-based glue, so in the end it is worth trying a tiny drop of distilled water again and again reinforced with steady patience.

5. When finished, leave to dry.

6. Next day you will see how little you have really removed and you must patiently work in tiny patches all over again. I once spent ten days on one fan alone, where every single fold was held together with stamp hinges, back and front, and every single pleat was split from one end to the other. It now looks perfectly normal, having been held together with Nylon Gossamer Fabric and Calaton and repainted in gouache.

Mending ivory sticks

1. Go to Friedleins and select off-cuts to match your own (cleaned) broken ivory stick. Elephant ivory can vary widely in tone and you must look out to see that the striations are running the right way. Equally, grain at right angles to grain can strengthen a joint as long as it looks right when completed.

2. Work your own ivory: it is not very difficult and makes a splendid hobby for a bed-bound invalid. In general, as Europeans normally tend to have done throughout history, work in paper-thin layers rather than the Oriental techniques of carving in the round.

3. Clean the ivory you are about to work with Pre-lim or Groom/stick and apply Mystox solution. After all, your "new" ivory has been lying for possibly years on the floor of some warehouse and before that has come from some hot country…in which case it would be strange if it was clean and free from mites.

4. Make a template in thick paper: in other words a matching pattern of the broken part from one of the other sticks. Unless both guards are broken you will have the other to copy from, and the same with the sticks. Make certain the stick you wish to replace is correct in shape. Never assume that all sticks are of uniform shape.

5. Stick the paper pattern on to the ivory and then quietly work away at cutting the surplus ivory to the correct shape. Use any tool which will help such as a knife, gouge, rasp, jeweller's saw, file or emery-board.

6. Allow at least half a day before you continue with the work, as a fresh eye can often see some slight flaws.

7. Slightly roughen the surfaces to be

stuck together and remember how tough ivory is…the last time that ivory might have been used could have been as a tusk in the jungle, lifting trees.

8. Use Araldite, following the instructions carefully, and then hold the mending pieces together (if necessary) with wooden clothes pegs and make sure that there is an even tension. Rest the other parts of the fan on or against something so there is no weight or stress on the repaired parts. NEVER use plastic clothes pegs: they stick for ever.

9. Leave the work on a piece of clean, waxed or greaseproof paper, having covered it with another piece, and holding the paper in place with either small weights or large bulldog clips to the table.

10. Leave for at least twenty-four hours.

Broken Tortoiseshell

Work in the same way as with ivory, taking even more care to match the colour. Buy all you may need at once as supplies are very low; even buy broken old fans with tortoiseshell sticks as they can be re-used with care.

Remember how marvellously the shell works under heat. Tortoiseshell can be moulded to any shape, once heated by steeping it in very hot water. It is also much easier to carve when hot, but remember how easy it is to remove just a fraction too much – for it cannot be replaced once cut.

If tortoiseshell is inlaid with, perhaps, gold initials or pique-work, take great care. Once the shell slightly expands when hot the gold or silver could pop out and it would be too difficult to replace.

Broken Mother-of-Pearl

This is a very difficult process; it is better, if possible, to buy some old and broken fans with the same type of pearl sticks and use them. In general one should never throw away one single fraction of old materials from fans. They should all be placed in containers which are clearly separated and marked (glass jars are best) and with a small bag of Silica Gel inserted, and left until they are needed.

Because of its structure mother-of-pearl can easily shatter. You have to work it with great care, very slowly, using a sawing motion, with a very fine rasp, file or jeweller's saw. Never attempt to pierce or perforate pearl; it is a specialist's job. However it is surprising how often guards and sticks in mother-of-pearl of the nineteenth century are similar, using the same pattern. So your own broken stick might be strengthened by backing one on to another. Or you can use a *small* new area to mend a stick, as long as its size does not interrupt the main pattern.

Use the same Araldite technique as with ivory. Always be careful to coat each side of the pearl evenly and then press together, holding with wooden clothes pegs, so that no small bubbles of air are trapped inside.

Broken wooden sticks

Many sticks of Western European fans are made from relatively soft fruit woods, such as laburnum, holly and pear. These sticks soak up liquids so should not be cleaned with water but either Vulpex in white spirit,

Groom/stick or Pre-lim, using dry cotton wool on a wooden cocktail stick.

Start by the rivet end; if it is possible to undo the rivet then your task is simple, otherwise you will have to take great care. Examine the rivet area to see whether there are any paper "sleepers" in between the sticks; sometimes there are and sometimes some of them have dropped out. They cushion the sticks from each other (especially in the case of mother-of-pearl) or they act as a buffer when there are only a few sticks, such as with a Battoir fan from Spain, having perhaps only eight sticks.

In making the fan originally, a good deal of attention was employed to keep its balance and weight correct – it would be hopeless to have a fan with a heavy satin leaf and only eight sticks held by a miniscule rivet…it would break up in a few hours. So the area by the rivet has to counterbalance the other end by the leaf, not only in weight but in visible thickness or thinness. To do so it has often become necessary to incorporate paper "sleepers" in between the sticks by the rivet. These may need to be replaced – ideally they always should, because they are sure to be dirty.

Then take your swab and cleaning agent (or Groom/stick) and begin working from the rivet away from your body towards the leaf. If the cocktail stick is too thick then you can use a darning needle with a wisp of cotton wool wound round it. Work carefully and evenly with a gentle sweeping motion. Change the cotton wool often (you will be surprised how many times you have to do so on every stick) and when you think you have done enough on one stick place a small wedge, like a piece of soft cotton wool, between it and the next. Start with the left-hand guard, then the first stick on the left, then let the next stick fall onto the first (with the cotton wool in between, not something hard or you could fracture the stick with the pressure of your fingers) and deal with that. Then the next, and so on, until you come to the right-hand guard at the end.

Leave your cleaned work for a day and then start on the other side in exactly the same way. Then do it all over again – you will be amazed at the amount which still needs to come off. After all, dirt is virtually always perspiration from the owner's hot hands (you don't use a fan in the cold) which is acid grease and dust which, apart from being distasteful, is also eating into the material of the sticks. The first time you clean you are virtually loosening the first layer of dirt – then you have to clean it properly; probably no-one else has done so for a hundred years or more.

Replacing a rivet (also useful for replacing a missing loop)

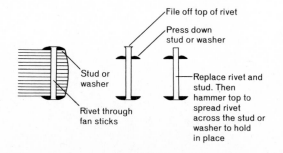

One of the reasons you must not use water is because during the Victorian age there was a craze for "do it yourself" – and that included painting and dyeing fan sticks. Water would then streak the sticks as the home-made dye or stain came off unevenly.

Apply Mystox solution as a fungicide to prevent mould, and finish with Renaissance wax polish to give the sticks a soft sheen. It is essential to turn again and again to the sticks, for clean sticks make a fan look wonderful but, however gorgeous the leaf, dirty sticks make a fan look foul.

Rivets

Rivets from really good fans unscrew, being virtually screws within tubes, with possibly a sparkling stone at each end. However they may not have been unscrewed for over a hundred years, and could be stiff with dirt or slight corrosion.

The best plan is to hold the fan up in the air with the rivet end pointing downwards and then apply ONE drop of 3-in-1 penetrating oil to each end of the rivet. DON'T lay the fan down, for the oil, taking the dirt with it, might slide up your sticks and stain both them and the leaf. Wait for a few moments and then gently try to unloosen the screw.

If you are successful (and your feelings of relief will be intense if you are) then still take care not to put the fan flat until you have cleaned away the oil and dirt. Hold the leaf end within a small plastic bag, so you can see what you are doing, and keep it upwards whilst you carefully wipe clean the rivet end and part of the sticks – penetrating oil really does penetrate and travels far farther than you would think.

You can then lay the fan flat and begin to clean it. When replacing the rivet into the cleaned sticks be careful to replace any small "sleepers" and also see that no penetrating oil is lurking inside the screw – in time it would work its way up onto the leaf.

The "sleepers" can be made from any small pieces of paper similar to the ones which have fallen out – old Christmas cards would do – with a six-way leather punch. Where Nylon Gossamer has been used to reinforce the whole leaf the small amount of leaf thickening which results will probably compensate for the loss of new "sleepers". But where mother-of-pearl decoration has been used it is safer to replace all missing "sleepers" to prevent pearled surfaces rubbing each other.

Many rivets do not unscrew but are rivets in the true sense of the word i.e. flattened ends. One end can be filed off and then everything comes to pieces for mending or cleaning. Replace everything and give the rivet a sharp tap or two on a hard surface, with a small hammer, to spread it over the washer again.

If you feel that this is too dangerous and you need help (especially if the rivet is silver) you could enlist the help of your local Do-It-Yourself shop and find out if there are any people in your area who work in metals: a gunsmith, a silversmith, a clockmaker or any other keen craftsman.

Finally you have to replace the ribbons onto your loop – otherwise there would be no point in having a loop at all.

Loops were added during the nineteenth century so that the fan might still be carried even though you now had so many other things to carry too. No longer did a little page walk behind you with everything you needed, you had to manage by yourself – a parasol, a reticule, possibly a band-box, leaving a hand free to shake the hand of the next acquaintance. So the fan had a loop added, and the loop was threaded with ribbons and then knotted about six inches down, so that your fingers could slip through the ribbon loop, the folded fan would hang close by your side within reach of your hand and the rest of the ribbons would flutter in the breeze.

It is best to have a length of ribbon which is just over twice the length of your fan. Fold the ribbon loop; the folded fan would hang through the loop, bring it through a few inches and then slip the two loose ends through the unbroken ribbon, pull it tight and it is secure. Then knot the two flying ends about six inches from the fan loop and cut the ends at an angle so that they will not fray. The width of the ribbon depends on the size of your fan; a tiny brisé fan would need ribbons which are strong enough to hold it safely but narrow enough not to swamp the fan. Similarly a large Victorian silk fan would need correspondingly wider ribbon, for wispy ribbons would look out of proportion.

The colours of ribbons are of importance. Naturally a black fan would have black silk or satin ribbons, and white would have white. But is the fan *really* white? It would be doubtful – it is more probably a creamy shade and dead white would look glaringly wrong. Painted fans are the problem; you have to pick out some shade within the scene which would also go with the type of fan, the type of occasion you would use it and the type of clothes you would wear with your fan. Pastel shades are usually best and

Re-ribboning through the loop of a fan

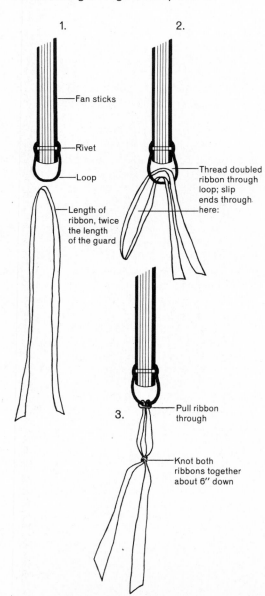

1.
— Fan sticks
— Rivet
— Loop
— Length of ribbon, twice the length of the guard

2.
Thread doubled ribbon through loop; slip ends through here:

3.
Pull ribbon through
Knot both ribbons together about 6" down

the palest of pinks should be left to teenagers.

A last word about ribbons on a nineteenth century fan – when using it for some occasion do see that the ribbons are pressed just before you go out…rumpled ribbons are a disgrace.

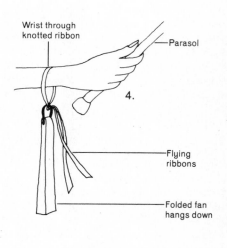

Wrist through knotted ribbon
— Parasol
4.
— Flying ribbons
— Folded fan hangs down

Foil on sticks

Coloured foil is always sandwiched between two thin layers of ivory or mother-of-pearl, placed against a flat backing section and highlighting a carved motif which has been fixed on top of the colour – it is a typical European technique and rarely used in the Orient.

In order to replace the old foil (the original was wafer thin and snapped when the fan struck, even lightly, some hard object ...or it was stretched too tightly when it was first applied) you have to separate the layers of ivory or mother-of-pearl. The best way is to use tiny drops of cellulose thinner on cotton-wool-wrapped cocktail stick, holding the remainder of the fan upwards and away from the thinner.

This is tricky to do, but you do not want cellulose thinner spreading all over the leaf of your fan, so it MUST be kept at an angle away from the guard or sticks. Gradually ease off the top layer of the guard sticks, then remove the old foil with eyebrow tweezers.

Clean the area very thoroughly and also clean the upper section at the same time. Replace the coloured foil with an adhesive and allow to dry quite thoroughly for a day before you place the upper section back on top of the foil.

If both guards need attention then it is best to prise open both before you think of replacing the foil – should only one part manage to come away it would be a great mistake to replace new foil on one side and leave the other empty or with old foil.

If you cannot prise apart the two sections (and they may take several days of treatment) then it is best to remove the old foil with eyebrow tweezers and just leave them alone except for cleaning everything.

Silvering

Real silver mounts, rivets, initials etc can be polished up with Silvo. Silver leaf, which might have turned black, cannot be polished or cleaned. It is about one thousandth of an inch thick, so using a liquid polisher would melt the fish or bone glue originally used as an adhesive and the silver leaf immediately slides off.

You then have to make up your mind whether you want to remove all the blackened silver leaf, to leave it free from decoration, or to fake new silver leaf. It's up to you.

If you want to replace the silvering effect then you must use a large magnifying glass, a strong light, very tiny paint brushes and an enormous amount of patience. Use a preparation like Rowney's Kandahar Silver and a tiny brush and work on the design with tiny brush strokes, remembering that curves and short strokes are easier to do than long straight lines.

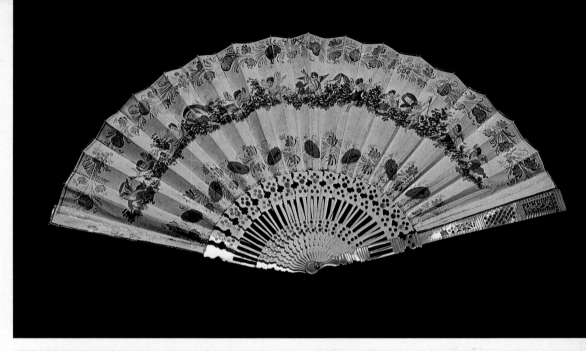
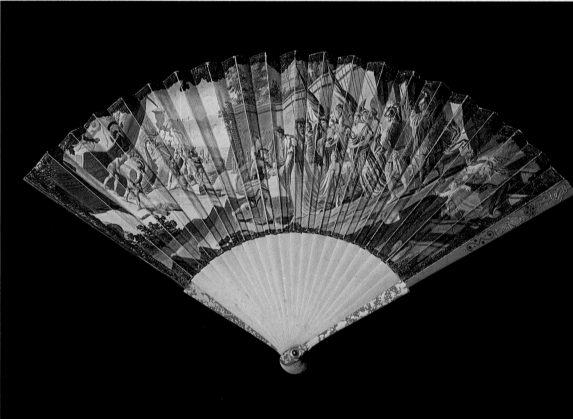

Top left. *Pink gauze Edwardian fan painted with a spray of cherry blossom. Pink-tinted mother-of-pearl sticks and guard.*
Top right. *Spanish fan, c. 1830, showing amorini painted on chicken-skin. The bone sticks are carved and have cut-steels piqué, the guards are of mother-of-pearl with insertions of small turquoises. The inscription on the reverse is "El amor consigue y la fortuna no." (Possibly printed in France.)*
Centre right. *Italian fan, c. 1730, showing "The Arrival of Aeneas". The sticks are of ivory, the ivory guards painted to simulate marble, with silver piqué-work and small figures from the Commedia del Arte in mother-of-pearl.*
Bottom right. *Empire fan, c. 1815. The leaf painted on chicken-skin, the sticks of pierced cut-steel; the guard has a mother-of-pearl insertion.*

Once you have finished the decoration on the fan sticks – which might take several days – leave the fan to dry off for a few days. Then take another silver preparation which is faintly different in tone and work along the same lines, but merely making an edge on the right hand side of the original lines – in other words you are providing a shaded effect, only about two hairs' breadth wide. This way the finished article looks more "genuine" than if you used merely one colour; the two-toned effect is a trick to make re-silvering look less new.

Gilding

The techniques are the same as with silver leaf, for you cannot work new gold leaf with any guaranteed success. Much depends upon the colour you want to produce. The American product Rub 'n Buff has at least a dozen shades of both gold and silver, including "antique" colours; Renaissance Liquid Leaf and Rowney's Liquid Gold Leaf are good and especially so is Goldfinger, which dries in half an hour and can be buffed up to a very high and durable polish. There are a great many other products to be found in good art shops as well.

I often use a little line of red paint to start with, then curve two different tones of gold round that, and it ends by giving a modelled effect as if the gold is in high relief.

Brush cleaning

Brushes should always be kept spotless and each washed in Polyclens Plus after use, followed by a bath of hot soapy water. Rinse thoroughly and then keep the brushes upright in a jar. Always buy the best quality brushes, for you will never regret it. When using gouache paints it is advisable to use a different brush for each colour, so you might as well begin by having about a dozen brushes for that alone.

When using either gold or silver I prefer to keep brushes just for these colours; however careful one is an occasional speck of gold or glint of silver gets into the next colour and is difficult to remove. Four jars for brushes is ideal; one for colours, one for silver, one for gold and one for applying touches of adhesives…and all should be labelled.

Repairing fan leaves

Repairing the leaf of a fan depends upon its condition. You have to decide whether you want to salvage the original material or start afresh with new material on old sticks.

If you do this it would be purely for your own pleasure: you could not, in all conscience, sell the fan afterwards. On the other hand, the sticks might be so beautiful that it would be a crime to throw them away – so a new leaf is viable. Conversely the sticks might be damaged beyond repair, yet the leaf in good condition, so the old leaf is then put onto new sticks.

Again, I must stress that if you do such a thing it could not really be sold UNLESS you had put all your cards on the table and told people what you had done.

It is always best to keep to the original material of the fan and, virtually, patch it. Once you have practised on some old and worthless fans you will find that you become so expert that few people will be able to detect any repair.

The commonest fault a fan can acquire is to have splits down the pleats from continual opening and shutting; this is the way to repair a fan in such a condition whether made from textiles, chicken-skin or paper.

1. Clean the fan sticks first, whatever they .re made from. A damaged fan will almost certainly be lifting at the edges of the material of the leaf, so it will not harm if you carefully clean right under the edge of the leaf, making the sticks look perfect.

2. Do not remove the leaf from the sticks; this would be utter madness and you would never, ever, get it back on again.

3. Prepare a pastry board or a similarly large, firm surface.

4. Pin clean white blotting paper all over it with drawing pins.

Below. *A handsome gold-coloured satin fan painted with sunflowers, with wooden sticks and guard. Almost certainly it would have flown contrasting green-coloured satin ribbon from the loop, for which it is made, tied about six inches down so that the fan could hang from the wrist when not in use.*

Top right. *An English textured fan, the leaf of thick, hand-made paper, delicately painted with flowers and punched with a design (sometimes the punching went right through the paper and was called 'decoupé' – this one is rarer). The sticks are of finely-carved plain ivory. c. 1780.*

Bottom right. *An early English fan, c. 1710, showing a painted scene of a music party. The round-shouldered ivory sticks show the traditional overlapping of the period.*

Overleaf. *An unusual pair of handscreen-fans made of painted, watered silk, with pure silk fringes and tassels and silk ribbon-covered wire handles. Made by Melles M & E Natté, Rio de Janeiro, Brazil. c. 1850.*

Top left. *English late 18th century fan. The silk mount is decorated with spangles and three stippled engravings printed in colour, after Bartolozzi. Pressed ivory sticks and guards carved with pagodas and other Chinese motifs.*

Bottom left. *Dutch (?) fan, c. 1745. The paper leaf is painted in tones of 'vieux rose' and shows a lady and a gentleman in a park, with a child playing the triangle. The top of the leaf decoupé, punched in a diamond motif. Ivory sticks are painted in deep pinks and silver.*

Right. *Unusual Empire fan with a silk leaf smothered with gold sequins and spangles (sequins are circular, spangles are shaped); the long sticks heavily carved and painted with flowers, the remainder left plain. Carved Oriental ivory sticks, leaf either French or English. c. 1810.*

5. Place the fan onto the board, which is lying flat, and then fix a large square of Filtration Fabric over the top of the fan. You can hold it in place with bulldog clips at the edges of the board or just use drawing pins to hold over the fan securely, but not too tightly.

6. Use a small hand vacuum-cleaner at some distance from the fan and allow the dust to suck up into the nozzle. Be careful not to clean too closely or tiny pieces of flaking leaf might disappear up the nozzle too.

7. Remove the Filtration Fabric and brush it off, for it can be used again and again.

8. Prepare some pieces of Nylon Gossamer Fabric into strips about one and a half inches wide – never wider – and about six inches long (depending on the length of your splits). Prepare sufficient for the entire work on the fan, this might be about thirty or forty pieces, it does not matter if you have too many as they can be used later for the other side or another fan.

9. Mix up a saucer of Cellofas paste.

10. With a clean paint-brush apply the Cellofas to the material you are mending and also to a strip of the Nylon Gossamer Fabric.

11. Place the strip over the area, gently pressing down with clean hands and holding the split areas together. Generously cover the area and overlap the joint by about one inch – to be cut away later.

12. Wash your hands.

13. Deal with the next split in the same way, overlapping where necessary.

14. Wash your hands between each split.

15. Keep the rest of the fan out of the way; weigh down guards or hold the fan on the board with either rustless pins or tiny weights covered in white blotting paper.

16. Leave for at least twenty-four hours.

17. When the fan is completely mended on the one side, trim the excess Nylon Gossamer Fabric from it, press down the edges with more clean Cellofas and then pleat the mended area between your fingers. Do NOT iron the material, but you can place a strip of greaseproof paper along the seams and put under some form of weight for the night, with the greaseproof paper both under and over the pleat as well.

18. Finish by painting in gouache paints the area you have mended. This is very easy as the Nylon Gossamer Fabric is transparent and you can see both the design and the depth of colour underneath. Trim the edges, see that the area by the sticks is secure with Cellofas again and apply gimp or whatever trimmings were there before. The Nylon Gossamer Fabric will then be invisible.

If no paints are needed you will find that the Nylon Gossamer Fabric will blend into whatever the background is just because it is almost transparent and has no weft or warp.

Mending a lace fan

First your lace fan has to be cleaned. As long as the fan has no sequins or spangles upon it you can carry out the techniques (stages 1–7 inclusive) of the section above.

Having removed your Filtration Fabric, and holding the fan with tiny rustless pins against the blotting paper, tip the board until it is almost upright. Then steam the fan with a kettle *held at least two feet away.* There are occasions when candle grease has spilled upon a lace fan and this is the only way to remove it safely. Do not allow the kettle any closer as some lace melts along with the grease into the blotting paper (and possibly has burnt under the grease anyway and the grease is merely holding it together – in which case a hole appears when the candle grease melts). This need not disturb you unduly and some sticks might buckle or paint disappear.

Leave the lace fan upon the blotting paper until it is quite dry. Then do the other side. You may have to do this several times, each side, before all the dirt and grease has been removed.

Do not worry about iron-mould marks – there is nothing at all you can do about them, so it is merely a waste of time to consider the problem. All you can actually do is to cover them up, generally with new spangles (the marks will have come from rusting sequins or spangles) or with mother-of-pearl sequins on white lace. These are opaque, so they do not show the marks below, and can be sewn into place with invisible thread. There is a difference between a sequin and a spangle.

Around the year A.D. 1280 the Venetians minted a gold coin named a "zechino"; it was small and pretty and worth a good deal. Several hundred years later the Venetians decided to withdraw the zechino, probably because it was too small for convenience. The ladies of Venice were furious, especially as they had saved nice little nest-eggs of zechini. So, in defiance one day, a lady decided to make a show of her now worthless coins. She made a hole in the centre of each and sewed all her hundreds of zechini to her spreading brocade dress – and twinkled all over the town. From then on ladies have worn sequins (as they came to be called) upon their dresses in order to catch the light and draw attention to themselves. Spangles, on the other hand, are not simple circular dots of metal, but shaped ones. Spangles are sophisticated sequins and can be in a multitude of shapes and materials, especially of cut steels.

If you decide that your lace fan leaf HAS to be washed this is how to go about it:-

1. Spread your fan onto a piece of clean blotting paper. Hold it in place with great care with tiny rustless pins, working from the centre outwards very evenly. By that I mean the centre of the fan leaf, taking the pins up against the central stick, then down to the edge by the sticks and rivet; then the next stick on either side, using six to eight pins along each stick and a final set all along the top edge. This means your fan is now securely and accurately held down on the paper. Now, using a fine pencil with a good sharp point, trace around the whole fan, marking every position of every stick.

2. Remove the fan from the board. Place clean waxed paper on the board so that no dirt can get onto it whilst you are washing the leaf.

3. Remove the lace from your sticks. This is best done over a contrasting surface below – white paper for a black fan, possibly blue blotting paper for a white fan and so on. Use a very sharp razor blade for the stitches – and extreme caution. One snick too far and you have a gratuitous hole. Do be careful NOT to keep old razor-blades; they are less than worthless once they are blunt, and once they are blunt they are wholly inaccurate. Warm water will probably remove the glues between the lace and the sticks.

Top left. *French fan, c. 1750, showing a well-painted scene of Bacchus and Ariadne, on paper. The sticks gilt in several shades of gold on mother-of-pearl, and with goldfish mother-of-pearl backing.*

Centre left. *Japanese Nanga fan. "Landscape, riverside hills with empty hut under trees", by Okada Hanko (1782–1846). Ink on paper. Inscription: "1844, summer; in the manner of Yün-lin; Hanko". Seals: 'Shuku-in', 'Hanko'.*

Bottom left. *Japanese folding fan. "Okame Flying on a Crane, Watching the Railway Train" (which was then newly introduced to Japan) by Kawanabe Kyosai (1831–89). Colours on paper. Signed: Shosho Kyosai. Sealed: artist's seal is in the shape of a sake bottle.*

Top right. *An Italian fan showing a mythological scene painted on vellum and having finely-carved ivory sticks showing cameos, clouté with mother-of-pearl and silver piqué. The guards are inlaid with Italian hardstones, clouté with mother-of-pearl and silver piqué. c. 1680–1700.*

Centre right. *18th century French (?) fan c. 1750. This shows a Pastorale painted on a paper leaf; carved, fretted and painted ivory sticks with an aquamarine pivot.*

Bottom right. *A fan dating from c. 1775, probably German. The leaf a hand-coloured etching of the "Judgement of Paris", in modern dress; the ivory sticks pierced and silvered.*

4. Clean the sticks and guards thoroughly. This might take a few days and other events might come up before you can go ahead with washing the leaf – so, although it sounds finicky to cover your original white blotting-paper with waxed paper it is well worth while in the end.

5. Wash your fan leaf in Vulpex Liquid Soap and distilled water. Hard water can leave a slight film on the lace, so it's best to play safe and use the distilled water.

6. Rinse in distilled water. One rinse should be enough because Vulpex Liquid Soap is non-foaming.

7. Pin the lace onto your original pattern on the blotting paper. Use just as many pins as you did in the beginning – even more if necessary and again taking great care to work from the centre outwards.

8. Allow the lace to dry for at least two days in an airy room but not in sunlight.

9. Replace the lace onto the sticks. Work from the centre outwards with two beading needles and invisible thread. I would tack it all on first, with large stitches, so you can see roughly if you are on the right stick area. Then take the same two needles and work with small stitches always taking care of the tension. Use short threads, finish off often. Attach the lace to the sticks in the way it was done in the beginning, but never work too tightly. Finally finish off at the edges and then use an adhesive, Evostik Clear, to hold down the lace by the guards.

10. You will now wish to mend any small holes there are. This can be done with Nylon Net. If the colour is incorrect – it is a creamy white when purchased – then you can dye it to whatever colour you want with a Dylon dye. Just a small portion of net will be needed and you ought to follow the directions with great care. Then cut out an irregular patch, perhaps to follow some design on the lace, and, with the smallest

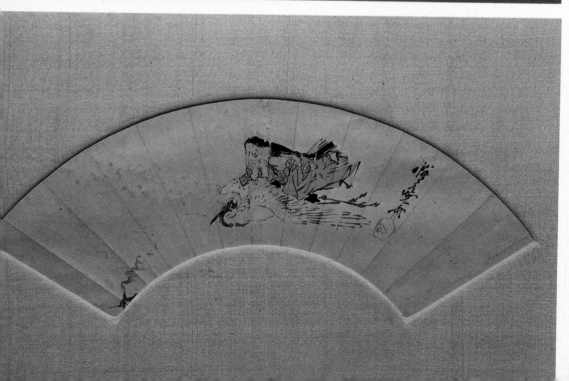

possible stitches and invisible thread, darn the net into place. It should be impossible to see.

11. Pleat the newly washed and mended lace with the fingers. It is sometimes possible to use a very fine spray of thinly mixed starch, or crispen with a two percent Calaton rinse along the edges of the folded lace fan to crisp up the pleats.

12. Leave for a day or two before opening up again.

Ostrich feather fans

These look formidable enough to deal with but they are really quite simple. Ostrich feather fans have generally three things wrong with them. They are either dirty, one or two spines of the feathers have broken or they would be improved by having the colour altered to match a new evening dress. Whichever the case you must always take the whole fan apart first. This is easy enough, the feathers have only been held on by a few cotton threads (as with pearl strings the threads need continually replacing to prevent lasting damage) and can be snipped apart.

1. Snip the threads of the fan.

2. Place the feathers in order upon a table; almost always they are of graduating sizes and so must be kept carefully on a surface and covered with some waxed paper, weighted down at the edges, so the feathers don't disappear onto the floor the moment the door opens and a draught sends them flying.

3. Deal with any trouble you might have with the sticks. If there is nothing wrong with them at least give them a thorough cleaning. Then apply Mystox LPL, finishing with Renaissance wax polish.

4. If the feathers are not too dirty then you can place them in some form of holder (you can use your own hand IF you wear gloves, you do not wish to be burnt by the steam) so

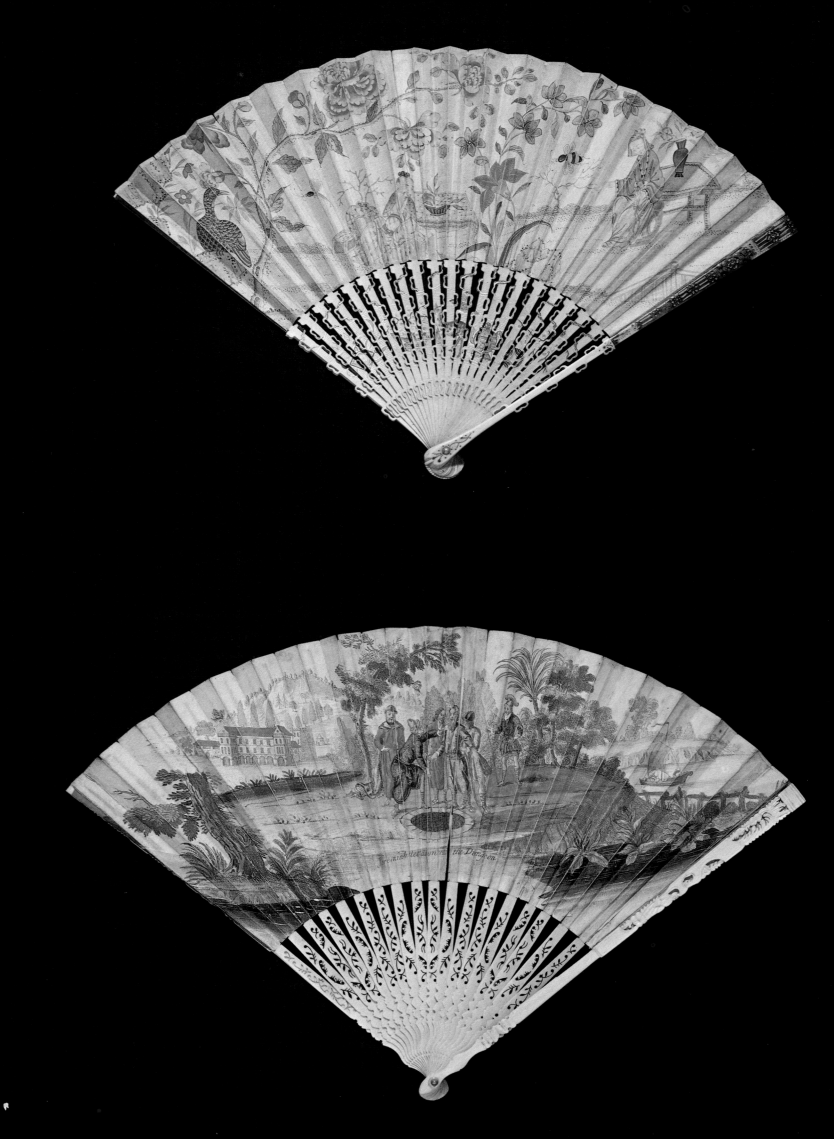

that the feather can stay upright steadily for several days…a large blob of Blutack will suffice.

5. Steam the feather about eighteen inches away from a kettle and then, whilst it is cooling down, curl the edges of the feather with a hot silver fork.

6. Leave for two days in its holder until quite dry.

7. If the feathers are very dirty then you can wash them – after all, ostriches go out in the rain. Do not use soap as it can so easily attract mould. Wash one feather at a time, having prepared your blobs of Blutack in advance. Use a bowl of warm distilled water and Vulpex, five percent is enough, and it will not make bubbles. Rinse in plain water until clear. Then, holding your feather up in the air (NEVER put it down on a surface while it is wet), you can use a hair-drier at "Warm" and give it a blow-dry, curving it in such a way that the feather turns in at the edges.

8. Put the dry feather into the Blutack holder and leave for a day.

9. To dye ostrich feathers in order to change their colour or to brighten them you can use any colourfast good dye for nylon. Follow the directions carefully and never allow the liquid to become too hot. Then dry out, as above, using a hair-drier at "Warm"; leave for two days in a Blutack holder.

10. Once your feathers are clean and ready you can put them back onto the sticks again, using either threads or adhesives where they were used before.

11. The method is to spread your fan sticks into a complete circle, so that when you are putting some adhesive (Evostik Clear is good) onto the spine of the feather in order to join it to the stick you will not have all the fronds of the previous feather sticking to it as well.

12. Glue one feather to a stick at a time. Leave to dry thoroughly, away from its companions. Allow plenty of time.

13. When all is dry you can thread the fan, using double invisible thread, and work from the left-hand guard first. Finish off the thread on each feather separately, so that if there is a break later on the whole fan need not be re-threaded.

14. Attach matching or contrasting ribbons to the loop; you must have the balance of flowing ribbons below an ostrich feather fan, otherwise it looks top-heavy.

N.B. If a feather has a broken spine you can pierce the base of the feather and run up inside it a piece of thick wire. Then bend the remaining three-quarters of an inch back onto itself, and blanket-stitch the spine with the wire inside.

Top left. *A Chinese fan which raises problems; one school of thought says it is dated c. 1740, another insists it is c. 1800. The ivory sticks are finely wrought; the guards have an addition of tortoiseshell.*
Bottom left. *A religious fan, printed, hand coloured and gilded, showing Jeremiah being led to the dungeon, and a topographical scene in the background. The sticks are of carved and pierced ivory. c. 1740. English.*

Re-threading ribbons

This question bedevils every fan collector, partly because of the difficulty of finding correct ribbons and partly because of the techniques. Miraculously I have, at last, discovered a firm which will sell ribbons fine enough and narrow enough for fans.

It is almost unfair to give their name, for people wish to buy such short lengths and that type of business would simply not pay these kind people. So, if at all possible, make a personal visit to London and go and see for yourself the widths, the prices and the types of ribbons available. Otherwise send too much money and they will work out the prices, the VAT, the postage and packing and return you your change. Their address is:
H. V. Caldicott Ltd., 20 Little Portland Street, London W.1. Manager Mr D. Curl.

They sell their ribbons by the roll, which has 250 metres on it. A group of enthusiasts might care to band together and buy a roll of "China" White (or Black) which starts at one eighth of an inch wide, with no woven border…this is perfect for a small ivory brisé fan. The price is $10 plus postage and packing.

They also sell French double satin, viscose single satin and nylon taffeta, in tiny widths and a multitude of colours. If, on the other hand, you only want a very short length to repair some ribboning, there are two substitutes:

1. Use very fine glove-leather in short strips of about one and a half inches at a time.

2. Better still, use Nylon Gossamer Fabric. Dip it into an aniline dye. When dry, cut it into strips about two inches long. Dip each strip into your Calaton mixture, hold two pieces together, squeeze through your finger and thumb and leave to dry. When dry the two pieces are bonded together; you can then trim them to the correct width and use. The Nylon Gossamer Fabric has no surface tension and will not exert any mechanical pressure on a fragile structure, so it is ideal for fans, especially the edges of a Vernis Martin brisé fan. The dye is to colour it to the shade you wish. One must remember that all ribbons in the past were not woven with a pattern but painted upon afterwards. You can now do exactly the same with your new ribbon.

3. Collect all the materials you are going to need together. That is: strips of bonded Nylon Gossamer Fabric. Invisible threads. Fine needles, preferably short ones. Tiny scissors. Eyebrow tweezers. The adhesive of your choice – Evostick Clear is good. A very strong light. A magnifying glass. Your sloping stand.

4. Work from the left-hand side. First of all fix a piece of short ribbon to the left-hand guard and then leave it for twenty-four hours. This is your anchor and must be completely firm before you start on the sticks.

5. Then you need to follow the method formerly used for ribboning your fan – every fan is different. Partly stick the ribbon to half your stick, partly sewing the next piece on with invisible threads, so that you get a type of box-like effect. Generally it is a case of glue to the far side of the stick, draw the ribbon through with your eyebrow tweezers,

position the stick over the first one so that the adhesive-bonded ribbon is invisible, and work on. Work in very small sections at a time.

6. A varnished brisé fan has to have the finest of ribbons, so the Nylon Gossamer Fabric type is ideal for this.

You start with sticking the ribbon fractionally to left of the central part of the top end of your ivory stick. Take it to the right, so that half of the top of the stick is now covered with fine ribbon. Then take the ribbon round to the back of the stick and stick it half way across the back. That means that just a little over half of every stick is covered in ribbon, half the front and half the back.

Then take your ribbon from the left-hand guard and bring it to the back of your stick, use an adhesive there, bringing it round to the front, also using an adhesive, so that now the whole stick is covered at the top, but with two separate pieces.

The left-hand one then travels on to the next stick (which you have already half-wrapped), but with a length in between which eventually acquires a fold in it, half way across. As the ribbon has to come from the centre of one stick to the centre of the next, yet show no daylight in between, the ribbon has to fold back onto itself. The first ribbon is taken round the stick, a little to left of centre and finished off a little to right of centre, so when the left-hand ribbon comes round to link it all together, it comes dead centre in each case, and you have no ugly gap of ivory where they meet.

To re-ribbon a Puzzle Fan

Puzzle fans are those which appear quite normal when opened up to the right and when they are opened up to the left they appear to fall apart. Generally Puzzle fans have two guards and nineteen sticks in between. The method is as follows:

1. Start the ribbon in the centre of the guardstick, pushing it into the wood. Most Puzzle fan guards are two layers, so that the ribbon lies inside securely. When the ribbon emerges it can travel either way as it comes out at right-angles.

2. There are three slits in stick No.1 (in fact in all the sticks) at even intervals across the stick. Take the ribbon from the guard, behind stick No.1, through the first slit, across the front, down through the second slit, across the back and out through the third slit. Glue to the remainder of the stick. Leave the ribbon hanging free for a while.

3. There are three slits in stick No.2. Take a new piece of ribbon and glue it on the back of the stick, in the centre, push it through the left-hand slit to come out at the front, push it back through the centre slit to arrive at the back, bring it through the third slit, to arrive back at the front, and let it hang loose.

4. Take the loose ribbon from stick No.1, which is hanging at the back, through to the first slit of stick No.3 and bring it from the back to the front; push it back through the second slit, to the back, back through the third slit, which brings it back to the front again, and use an adhesive, glueing the ribbon back onto the stick in the direction of the centre slit. Cut off ribbon.

5. Take the ribbon from stick No.2, by-

pass stick No.3 completely, bringing the ribbon in front of it and then behind stick No.4. Thread this ribbon through from the back of stick No.4, through the first slit, across the front of the stick, down through the middle slit to the back and back again through the third slit to the front and leave hanging.

6. Take a ribbon and start it again in the centre of stick No.5, glueing it to the back of stick No.5 and bringing it out through the first slit to the front, pass it across the front, back through the second slit in the centre, and back through to the front again – and then let this hang loose as it is going to by-pass stick No.6.

7. Take the ribbon hanging in the front of stick No.4 and by-pass stick No.5 completely, bringing the ribbon behind stick No.6, pass it through the first slit to the front, then through the centre slit to the back, then through the third slit back to the front again and use an adhesive on the last fraction, securing it down back towards the centre slit. Cut it off.

8. Take the ribbon hanging from the front of stick No.5, by-pass stick No.6, take it to the back of stick No.7, bring it through the first slit, pass it back through the centre slit, back through the last slit and then leave it to hang, as it is now going to by-pass stick No.8.

9. With stick No.8 start in the centre of the back, stick the ribbon from the centre slit across to the left-hand slit, pass it through to the front, back through the centre, back through to the front and then leave to hang free as this ribbon is going to by-pass stick No.9.

10. The ribbon hanging free in front of stick No.7 now by-passes stick No.8, goes (from the back) through the first slit of stick No.9, across the front, back through the centre, across the back, out through slit No.3 and is stuck on the surface of the stick, travelling left towards the centre slit. Cut off.

11. The whole performance is then repeated from 1 to 10, with the final ribbon being drawn into the last guard, so that it goes in at right-angles and has no general method of travel, either from right or from left.

12. This fan then looks perfectly natural when it is opened from left to right, but when it is opened from right to left it falls into seven distinct sections of three or four sticks at a time and looks as though the ribbon is entirely broken. You then carefully open it back from left to right and it is "mended" all over again.

Top left. *"The Language of the Fan", an advertising fan for "Old Spice" gentlemen's toiletries. c. 1910.*
Centre left. *A souvenir fan for the Eton and Harrow match at Lord's Cricket Ground, London, in 1870, showing the list of players for each team. The reverse advertises Rimmel's perfumes.*
Bottom left. *A sturdy advertising fan for the Restaurant Tabarin, Montmartre, Paris, showing this cartoon on the reverse. 19th century.*
Right. *Two Viennese fans made of painted wood. c. 1860.*

It is time-taking but can be made from ordinary wood, painted on the obverse with some large "Victorian" design, left plain on the reverse – and it sells well. The trick is not only the tension of the ribbons but that about seven eighths of the stick is exposed when opened out, left to right, giving those ribbons room to manoeuvre.

Re-ribboning simple fans
Type 1
Where there are three slots in the sticks and one can use a continuous ribbon. Always make sure that there is plenty of ribbon left at each end so adjustments might be made.

Start from the left, with the right (or obverse) side of your fan facing upwards: First stick; under, over, under – then over next stick. Repeat to the end. Adjust your tension accurately and then fasten your ribbon onto each guardstick. Now and then a few spots of glue will help to hold the tension accurately.

Type 2

Where there is only one slot in each stick.

Cut your pieces of ribbon to the width of two sticks; you will need the same number of pieces of ribbon as the number of your sticks plus one. You will also need two end pieces (which fix onto the guards) which equal the width of three sticks.

Start from the left, the wrong (or reverse) side of the fan facing upwards. Take a long piece of ribbon under first half stick, through the slot and glue on top. Do all the sticks right across the fan in the same way.

Then turn the fan over, fasten the second long ribbon to the guard, under the half-stick, through the slot and fasten under the next piece of ribbon. A pin will help to get the ribbon through, with possibly the additional help of a pair of eyebrow tweezers.

Repeat until all the sticks are joined and the last piece is fastened to the guard. Be very careful to adjust your tension as you work along.

A practical solution for a broken Victorian fan

We were once sent a very precious Victorian fan to mend – precious only in a sentimental light. It had been made c.1860, had a double

Top left. *Italian fan, fine parchment leaf painted with a "Judgement of Paris" in gouache. Fine, pressed ivory sticks and guards. c. 1795.*
Top centre left. *Venetian fan showing "The Exodus from Egypt" in the manner of Bellini. Finely pierced ivory sticks and guards. c. 1740.*
Bottom centre left. *Chinese folding fan. Ink on gold-flocked paper. "After the Mi family manner; inking this, again for respected elder Shih-kung; Ch'ing-sheng". Seals: 'Ch'ing' and 'Sheng'. This painting is high quality and probably dates from the early 17th century.*
Bottom left. *Japanese Nanga fan: "Peonies and Grasses" by Osada Buzen (1734-1806). Ink, gold and light touches of colour on paper. Signature: Buzen. Seals: two of the artist.*
Top right. *Black silk chiffon fan, English, painted in gouache with daisies. The wooden sticks were probably imported from Malaya. c. 1880.*
Bottom right. *Modern Spanish fan. c. 1978.*

Left. *A pet monkey and a full-face mask on a dressing table, painted by Hogarth, in "A Harlot's Progress". Courtesy of the Museum of Fine Arts, Boston, U.S.A.*

Right. *Miss Esther Oldham, the American Patron of the (International) Fan Circle. In the background are some of the renowned De Witt Clinton Cohen collection of fans which she acquired. The Oldham Collection's 16th century fan is seen at the right-hand top corner. Miss Oldham has recently donated her famous collection of fans to museums, mainly the Museum of Fine Arts in Boston.*

Below. *Mrs Doris Langley Moore O.B.E., F.R.S.L., Patron of the Fan Circle and founder of the Costume Museum in Bath, at the Inaugural Reception.*

Bottom right. *The Countess of Rosse, Patron of the Fan Circle and owner of the Messel Collection, with Mr Leslie Ross Collins, Master of the Worshipful Company of Fan Makers in 1975, looking at Lady Rosse's famous Autograph Fan at the Inaugural Reception of the Fan Circle in Fan Makers' Hall.*

It is documented that the *Beggar's Opera* played in New York in 1750.

The Old Theatre in New York in 1733 was replaced in 1750 by a "fine, large, and commodious new theatre where the old one stood, permission being granted the London Company in that year."

Mrs Lewis Hallam, a relative of John Rich, the first Producer in London of the *Beggar's Opera*, played a part in the New York production.

This fascinating and 'curious' mask fan, created by Hogarth, and advertised in the Boston News Letter in 1728 and so closely associated with the *Beggar's Opera*, is the most sought-after fan today as few have survived the wear and tear of nearly 250 years!

First published in Great Britain 1978 by Colour Library International Ltd.
© Colour Library International Ltd. 1978
Text © Nancy Armstrong 1978
Colour Separations by FERCROM, Barcelona, Spain
Text and filmsetting by Focus Photoset Ltd., London
Printed and bound by RIEUSSET, Barcelona, Spain
All rights reserved
ISBN 0-8317-0952-9
MAYFLOWER BOOKS